NEAR CHRISTIANITY

Near Christianity
Sorting Myth From Truth

Alistair Brown

Hodder & Stoughton
LONDON SYDNEY AUCKLAND

First published in Great Britain 1996

The right of Alistair Brown to be identified as the Author of the Work has been asserted by him in accordance with the Copyright, Designs and Patents Act 1988.

10 9 8 7 6 5 4 3 2 1

British Library Cataloguing in Publication Data
A record for this book is available from the British Library

ISBN 0 340 64238 6

Typeset by Hewer Text Composition Services, Edinburgh
Printed and bound in Great Britain by
Cox & Wyman Ltd, Reading, Berks

Hodder and Stoughton Ltd
A Division of Hodder Headline PLC
338 Euston Road
London NW1 3BH

For my Dad, among whose gifts to me
has been an enquiring mind

Contents

Acknowledgments

Alison's love, support, companionship and willingness to sacrifice is an essential and irreplaceable foundation for all I do. She also has an amazing gift for helping me see and correct errors in my work without damage to my male ego. I'd have married her for that alone. Without her this book could never have been done.

Our special friend Jane has been an indispensable help by entering all my editing changes in the manuscript. Most chapters had more changes than original writing, but she ploughed through them all with incredible accuracy. It took much time and much dedication. Now it's over we're planning to re-introduce her to her patient husband Ian.

Many others have given me encouragement and help, especially some very caring friends in Gerrard Street Baptist Church, Aberdeen. As this book is published, I'm preparing to move south to be the General Director of the Baptist Missionary Society, but the love and support of church members in Aberdeen will live with me always.

Finally, Catherine, Judith, Rachel and Alistair have helped me smile, kept me sane, dragged me away every now and again to watch TV, and often let me know I matter whatever my theology is like.

To all these I owe an immense debt of gratitude. Thank you.

Alistair Brown

Introduction

To climb Ben Nevis, the highest mountain in Britain, was a challenge I should have resisted, but in a moment of folly didn't. To go up and down took nearly ten hours of relentless slog. The fine mist which enveloped our family for two-thirds of our expedition had more than a passing resemblance to rain. We were soon exhausted, soaked to the skin, and wondering what kind of madness had possessed us to set out.

But at least we had gone prepared: boots, fleeces, jackets, maps, compass, sandwiches, soup and countless bars of chocolate. All we lacked were the crampons for the ice field near the top, but we hadn't expected that in August.

Were madness to strike us twice, and we re-climbed Ben Nevis, we would be wiser in what we took with us. More accurately, we'd leave a lot of gear behind. Certainly many items of clothing and equipment were vital, and we'd pack them again. Other things, though, were less necessary, and some were a positive encumbrance. So, for example, boots we needed, and soup was nice, but two guide books, ten apples and several extra sweaters only hindered our progress. We'd have done better without them.

Our Ben Nevis expedition is a parable for my view of evangelicalism today. As a card-carrying evangelical, I regard many doctrines as vital. Christ's deity, forgiveness through his death on the cross, the resurrection, Jesus's eventual return; these and plenty more are indispensable. I'm ready to negotiate fine details, but I can't miss any of these from my rucksack as I head for my spiritual summit. There are other things which are in the 'nice to have' category for evangelicals. Among those are being at church twice on a Sunday, at least thinking about tithing, memorising John 3:16 and Revelation 3:20, and knowing the four spiritual laws. It's probably good to take these things with me, even though I could probably manage my ascent minus them.

Then there are encumbrances, the excess baggage of evangelicalism. Actually, we didn't pack most of these into our rucksacks. They were there already. Generations of past evangelicals preprepared our rucksacks, and they were hoisted already full on to shoulders which didn't feel the strain in the early days. But our pilgrimage as Christians is hard work. We get weary. Perhaps the superfit don't care how much they carry, but the ordinary mortal finds even the smallest burden is one too many. The answer must be to jettison our excess baggage, and that does not mean only the outright heresies but also the near-truths of Christianity.

The issue is not merely one of comfort. Although some of the evangelical myths in this book may seem trivial, in fact they're hardships and hold Christians back. Faith is spoiled. Good people think, 'I ought to believe that, but I can't. Surely I'm not much of a Christian.' They get demoralised and largely ineffective, simply because they can't manage to believe something they should never have been asked to believe. Others haven't the self-discipline or ability to master the niceties of evangelical practice. 'I ought to read more, pray more, witness more . . . But I've tried so many times. I'll never get there. What a failure I am.' Self-condemnation is never good. It's doubly bad if the only failure is to satisfy what evangelical folklore has prescribed. With quite enough discouragement over genuine issues, we could do without more over unreal ones.

So my aim is to lighten your load by getting some evangelical myths out of your rucksack. Far from robbing

you of any spirituality, with these gone you'll be free to go
forward and find the realities of the Christian faith and life.
It'll still be hard. But at least you'll be facing the struggle
only on things that matter.

1

I know I'm in the will of God when I have peace in my heart

No one was sure which had been there longer, the Bible College or Professor George. Both by now were institutions, the latter held in the highest regard by colleagues and students alike. Not only was he a good scholar, but a man whose years had taught him many lessons. His wisdom was much sought after.

A young man came looking for Professor George's wisdom. He explained that he felt something special about the new female student who had joined his New Testament class.

'Do you mean the very pretty one with blonde hair?' asked the Professor.

The student was taken aback that such a venerable old professor would notice how attractive the new student was. But he was right. She was stunning. Not that that was why he felt anything special about her, he explained. It went deeper. In a way he found hard to explain, he knew she was the one God had singled out to be his wife. How did he know? He had a deep peace in his heart about her. This had to be the will of God.

The professor said some wise things, giving a mixture of encouragement and caution.

Next day there was another young man at his door. This student explained there was a new female student in his class, and he felt something special about her.

'The pretty blonde one?'

The student was astonished. This was a remarkable word of knowledge the professor had had, and confirmed what he already knew, that this was a girl marked out for him by God. He'd already felt that, for he had a deep peace about her in his heart.

Some more wise things were said by the professor, again with a mixture of encouragement and caution, this time with a little more emphasis on the caution.

The third day produced a third student wanting the professor's counsel. Professor George could have written his script for him. There was a new young student in his class – yes, the pretty one with blonde hair – and he felt she was special, the one God wanted him to marry. He was sure, for God had given him a deep peace in his heart about her.

Many wise things were shared with the young man, with much caution and hardly a hint of encouragement.

Unless God has decided that monogamy is unnecessarily restrictive for pretty blondes, not all these young men were right in interpreting their inner peace as God's leading. Yet a feeling of peace is precisely the proof of God's guidance for which many Christians look. It's the basis for countless decisions.

The first time they saw round it, Brian and Marion knew the brand new bungalow was the home for them. 'We had an overwhelming sense of peace,' they said. This was not entirely surprising since it was beautifully built, lavishly decorated and nestled prettily against a background of trees and fields. Their sense of peace was proof enough of the rightness of a move, and, though the cost was high, they bought the bungalow. Unfortunately they had difficulty selling their previous home, and special loans were needed for several months until they did. It cost them a fortune.

The youth club leadership was proving tough work for David. He'd started with great enthusiasm, but it was an enthusiasm which masked a touch of naïveté about how willing young people are to be led. He'd quickly discovered they liked their own ideas better than his, that even Christian young people are not automatically godly, and that there are more letdowns than successes. I tried to raise his spirits. Young people's work was always hard, and these youngsters would respond to him in time. Patience was what was needed. He listened, but didn't seem helped. A few weeks later he told me, 'Pastor, I feel it's right to stand down from being youth club leader.' I groaned. He'd been in the post only a few months, and there was no one else who could take over. Before I could stop myself, I'd pointed that out to him. David wasn't daunted. 'I know, but I don't have any real peace in my heart about carrying on with this job. It can't be the right thing for me.'

These days the presence or absence of a deep, inner peace is many people's way of getting guidance. Should it be? Is a feeling of deep inner peace the way to know the will of God?

Peace is the disciple's inheritance

Certainly many biblical characters experienced peace of one kind or another. Sometimes that was physical peace: 'And the kingdom of Jehoshaphat was at peace, for his God had given him rest on every side' (2 Chr. 20:30). Sometimes peace was psychological, like the reassurance Eli was able to give Hannah about having a child: 'Go in peace, and may the God of Israel grant you what you have asked of him' (1 Sam. 1:17). Sometimes peace is expressed in terms of being right with God: 'Great peace have they who love your law, and nothing can make them stumble' (Ps. 119:165).

God, in fact, is the 'Lord of peace' (2 Thess. 3:16), and the prophesied Messiah the 'Prince of Peace' (Isa. 9:6). His disciples, therefore, have an inheritance which includes peace: 'Peace I leave with you; my peace I give you. I do not give to you as the world gives. Do not let your hearts be troubled and do not be afraid' (John 14:27). Similarly,

Paul lists peace as coming from the Holy Spirit: 'The fruit of the Spirit is love, joy, peace, patience, kindness, goodness, faithfulness, gentleness and self-control' (Gal. 5:22–3).

These and many other Scripture passages describe peace as a prized possession of God's people. It seems reasonable, then, to make peace a guiding principle for decision-taking. 'Let the peace of Christ rule in your hearts' (Col. 3:15). Whatever promotes a sense of peace is right. Whatever robs us of peace must be wrong.

Yet the hard truth is that some decisions based on a sense of peace don't work out. None of the young men who thought the new student was God's choice of a wife for him was right. All three were rejected and tumbled into emotional heartache and spiritual confusion. Brian and Marion's pursuit of their new bungalow brought them to the verge of financial catastrophe. David's resignation as youth leader caused the youth club to close down.

What goes wrong? How can mistakes be made when people are striving simply to follow their sense of peace?

Many types of peace

Problem number one is having just one concept of what it means to be at peace. Many, especially in our hedonistic culture, think of being at peace only in terms of a sense of well-being, a warm glow inside.

The three Bible college students felt a warm glow – actually, more like a red hot glow – when they saw the new student. Brian and Marion felt maximum well-being about the luxury bungalow. David, by contrast, felt nothing but frustration about youth leadership. Every one of them was equating personal peace with 'I feel good inside'.

It *can* mean that, of course. But not only that, for the word peace has many meanings.

Probably our main use of peace is to refer to the opposite of war. It can similarly describe the golden silence after the children are finally asleep. Most often peace describes subjective feelings: harmony with a friend, tranquillity while gazing over a pastoral landscape, satisfaction from accomplishing something important, contentment after a good meal, confidence for the child whose hand is held firmly by an adult in a busy crowd, security of mind for the person who knows his financial investments are safe.

A more complex psychological meaning is peace which equates to a sense of rightness. An employer sacks a lazy or dishonest worker. Or a prosecuting lawyer presents evidence which results in a violent thug being jailed.

In situations like these a sense of peace may exist only deep down. The employer may be hurt by insults from the departing worker, or by criticism from other staff who don't know all the facts. Condemnation is discouraging. No one enjoys hearing it. Yet, if the employer really believes in the rightness of his decision, he's still at peace. The lawyer may have gone through the trial with threats hanging over him. An anonymous note told him that if he presented the prosecution case, his house would be burned down, his children kidnapped, or even his life terminated. Faced with such intimidation only the superhuman would not feel anxious. Yet he cannot compromise his principles. He will not deliberately 'throw' the case. To go on, and especially to win a guilty verdict, is high risk for him, but it's the right course of action. So he brings out every last shred of evidence. Only with justice done can he be at peace, even though outwardly he may face trouble.

So, the word peace means more than merely a strong feel-good factor. Sometimes even with a feel-bad factor a person would still be at peace.

True and false peace

Problem number two arises when a simplistic sense of peace directs decisions.

I'm stretched out on the couch, taking no greater exercise than my finger flicking the TV remote control to change channels. No one's bothering me, and life feels good. I'm at peace. My wife is being left to do all the housework while I laze around. Is it okay for me to be at peace? She certainly doesn't think so!

In that scenario, what I have is peace, but not of the best kind. A distinction must be made between true and false peace. The Bible recognises that. For example, those who give no thought to God but simply chase prosperity may have peace, but it's not a peace that God gives. 'They have no struggles; their bodies are healthy and strong. They are free from the burdens common to man; they are not plagued by human ills. This is what the wicked are like – always carefree, they increase in wealth' (Ps. 73:4–5; 12).

Such false peace isn't the experience only of those out of contact with God. Even Christians can be complacent in its comfort. Jesus warned the church at Laodicea, 'You say, "I am rich; I have acquired wealth and do not need a thing." But you do not realise that you are wretched, pitiful, poor, blind and naked. Those whom I love I rebuke and discipline. So be earnest, and repent' (Rev. 3:17, 19).

False peace is a widespread disease. The drug baron who assassinates all his rival suppliers could feel at peace. The unfaithful husband who considers guilt an outmoded concept could feel at peace. The drunkard who is past caring that he's lying in the gutter could feel at peace. The peace these people have is real enough, but it's not a good peace. It's not the kind of peace Jesus gave!

Thus, a feeling of peace can be generated by *either* bad actions *or* good actions. Adolph Hitler felt at peace exterminating Jews; Dietrich Bonhoeffer felt at peace opposing Nazism. If the only measure of rightness was a sense of peace, both would have their actions legitimised. Yet not both were right.

A subjective feeling of peace is an inadequate guide to what's right. The Bible college students with matrimonial ambitions, the couple who wanted the bungalow, the youth leader who wanted tranquillity, all were being ruled by the simplistic definition of peace identified earlier: superficially feeling good. When that was there, they assumed they were in the right. When it wasn't there, they assumed they were in the wrong. Decisions based on feeling good were inevitably self-indulgent.

The truth about peace is harder.

Unmentioned biblical teaching about peace

First, Jesus never promised anyone superficial peace. 'Do not suppose that I have come to bring peace to the earth. I did not come to bring peace, but a sword' (Matt. 10:34). 'Do you think I came to bring peace on earth? No, I tell you, but division' (Luke 12:51). Are these strange words from the Prince of Peace? Only if we think of peace in superficial terms. The truth is that the peace Jesus gives his disciples is far deeper than superficial feelings and circumstances.

Second, Jesus taught self-denial as essential for anyone who would be a Christian. 'Then he called the crowd to him along with his disciples and said: "If anyone would come after me, he must deny himself and take up his cross and follow me"' (Mark 8:34). Self-denial hurts. No one who follows Jesus can be ruled by what superficially feels good.

Third, Jesus specifically distinguished between the hardships this world would bring his disciples and the peace they would find through their relationship with him. 'I have told you these things, so that in me you may have peace. In this world you will have trouble. But take heart! I have overcome the world' (John 16:33). So, a Christian could be perfectly in the will of God but experiencing perpetual problems, pain or persecution. Life would be difficult and perhaps feel wretched, but deep in his spirit the believer would be at peace.

Fourth, Jesus talked of peace at exactly the same time that he was commissioning his disciples for hard and dangerous work. 'Peace be with you! As the Father has sent me, I am sending you' (John 20:21). They knew the risks. They were hiding behind locked doors because just days earlier they had seen Jesus crucified. They could expect little better if they carried on his work. On the surface, they must have shuddered at Jesus's command. But deep inside they knew this was right, that they would be given strength from God, and so they had peace.

Decisions made on a superficial sense of peace reveal ignorance of all four of these biblical truths. Guidance based on a self-indulgent definition of peace promotes personal contentment to the status of a god. Whatever pleases it is right; whatever displeases it is wrong.

That's not biblical. We cannot be led by a false god.

The peace of Christ

The peace we are to honour, Paul said, is the peace of Christ. That means having peace like his. Jesus didn't always feel good. He wept at the grave of Lazarus (John 11:35), cried in pity or despair over Jerusalem (Luke 13:34), and was in such anguish in Gethsemane that his sweat was like drops of blood (Luke 22:44). Those were hard times, but he accepted them because his sense of peace rested on his relationship with his Father and doing his will, not on outward events or superficial feelings. He knew he was loved by his Father (John 5:20), and he lived to please him: 'I seek not to please myself but him who sent me' (John 5:30); 'I have come down from heaven not to do my will but to do the will of him who sent me' (John 6:38). Jesus sacrificed self-comfort and self-interest out of obedience to his Father. That way – only that way – was he at peace.

Those ruled by Christ's peace will do the same. For them, as for Jesus, only knowing God and doing his will, even if it includes a cross, can bring real peace. Any other peace, no matter how attractive, is a false leader. Following it may take us far from God's plan for our lives.

With our son nearing one year old, Alison and I knew the

time had come to move home. All three of us were sharing a bedroom so small we had to take turns to get undressed. Where would we go? We could probably afford another flat a little larger. We hoped it could be on the better side of town, nearer our church, nearer our friends. We began the search.

Then Harry appeared. He'd just been appointed pastor of a tiny struggling congregation in a massive public housing scheme. It was one of the largest and most deprived schemes in the whole of Europe, riddled with drugs, violence and vandalism. Harry had been given our names, and had come to ask us for help. Us? We belonged to the poshest church in town and wanted to stay there. We prayed God would give Harry other helpers while we kept searching for houses in nice areas.

But it didn't work. Harry's plea for help began to bug us seriously, and in strange ways we were getting nowhere trying to buy houses. The final straw was when a house we wanted was advertised at a fixed price – we offered that price – and our offer was refused. We took God's hint. With a million misgivings, I wrote a letter to the local authority asking them to rent a property to us in the housing scheme. I think we became the first family ever who asked to move *into* that area.

A home was allocated, and we went to look at it. It was in one of the roughest streets, its windows boarded up, and sinister-looking teenagers lounged about the common stair. At least the neighbours didn't peek at us from behind their curtains. They opened their windows wide, leaned out and stared. Inside, the place was spartan, apart from an impressive collection of droppings on top of a cupboard where the previous tenant had kept his pigeons. From upstairs blared Jim Reeves at a volume which threatened damage to our hearing, never mind to the person in whose apartment the records were being played.

Someone we loved dearly heard of our plans and said she'd never visit if we lived there. That hurt. But we knew the place was right, and told the housing authority we'd take it.

Tradesmen removed the boards from the windows only an hour or two before we moved in – any earlier was to invite theft and vandalism. Once we were installed we found the other occupants or, rather, they found us – mice and fleas. The land outside was strewn with refuse; the neighbours were noisy; some friends were too frightened to visit; the Christian work was unbelievably hard. So much about being there was difficult. Many things would have been easier, more comfortable, somewhere else.

Yet, despite it all, we grew to be so happy in that place. Nowhere else would have been right. Knowing that, and knowing the safest place in the whole world is the centre of God's will, we had peace.

If we'd made *our* peace the goal, we'd never have gone to live in that scheme. Our peace didn't take us there. We had to unravel God's plans other ways, based on other criteria, some ordinary, some extraordinary. Having found them and having obeyed, God granted us that deep treasure of *his* peace.

2

It's what you believe that
makes you a Christian

A thousand thoughts danced through the young man's mind as he sat hunched in front of his gas fire, staring at the flames. Perhaps being only eighteen years old was young to have a crisis, but this felt like one. All his life he'd been around Christians. His thoughts flitted back to church services as a child, and carving his initials in the varnish of the pew when the long prayer was just too long. In Sunday School he had coloured innumerable pictures of a handsome, blond, remarkably white-skinned Jesus. Sermons had left him amazed, amazed that adults could find them interesting, or did their fixed stares towards the front have another explanation? He remembered the church picnics with their squashed sandwiches, anaemic orange juice and races in which he always came first at the wrong end. There were the socials which were somehow unmissable events for everyone, where he'd played his violin and Christian grace in the audience had summoned him back for an encore. There were the evangelistic rallies with a call to make a decision, and the expectation that by now he would have done so. But he never had. The flames flickered. His mind was a disturbing blend of confusion and despair.

It was Irene's question at the youth group meeting the previous night which had brought on the crisis. 'What do Christians mean when they say Christ died for them?' The moment she'd asked that an icy shiver had run through the young man. That was it. All these years – so many lessons, sermons, hymns – and he didn't know the answer. Over and over he'd heard the phrase 'Christ died for us', but he didn't know what it meant. Now he had to know. He had to get the answer.

He prayed, 'God, help me to understand about Jesus . . .' Prayer wasn't new. He'd always believed in God. It seemed to make better sense than to think everything about the world happened by accident. But why was Jesus necessary? If God wanted to forgive people, why couldn't he just do it? Why send his Son? Why put him on a cross?

Time slipped past. It was after midnight now, and the night chill crept into the young man's bones. He pushed another couple of coins in the meter to keep the fire going. 'Please God,' he prayed, 'I've got to know. I've got to understand.' But he couldn't. He didn't lack ideas, but they were scattered through his thoughts like a thousand pieces of a jigsaw with none fitting together.

One o'clock came and went. Again and again the question, 'What do Christians mean when they say Christ died for them?' Still no revelation, no comprehension, no answer. More and more, harder and harder he prayed. Through clenched teeth he begged God. 'Please, I *must* know . . . I *must* know . . .' On and on he searched through all he'd been told by parents, by ministers, by teachers. There had to be something there. More prayer. His heart pounded and sweat poured. 'God, show me . . .' From heaven, though, only silence. The thoughts refused to gel; insight would not come.

Exhausted, the young man sank back in his chair. The clock showed 2.30. He had an early start at work the next morning. He would have to get some sleep. Frustrated and disappointed, he gave up on his quest. The fire was switched off, clothes discarded, and a weary figure crawled into bed.

In an instant his brain was charged through as if with

spiritual electricity. New thoughts flashed to and fro. *Jesus showed exactly what God was like. He taught about him and lived precisely the way God wanted. He did everything God said.* A new line of logic was coming together. *When he came to Jerusalem he knew there were enemies who wanted to kill him. He could have walked away. He could have gone back to Galilee, hidden there, and had a quiet and safe life. But that would have meant backing down on everything he taught. He would have undone everything he'd already told the people. So he stayed in Jerusalem. He knew what would happen. He knew they'd arrest him and crucify him. But still he stayed. He wanted everyone to know the truth about God. He wanted me to know the truth. So he didn't run. He chose to die. He died for me . . .*

It took only seconds for those thoughts to come together, along with an overwhelming sense of God's presence and an irresistible need to make a decision for or against this Jesus. He had to choose at that moment to be a Christian or to forget the whole business. It would mean either giving God his whole life or never even going to church again. Light blazed through his brain. What Christ had done suddenly seemed clear. Deep in his inner spirit the young man decided 'yes'. Five minutes later he was asleep.

It was the beginning of a new life. Within days friends and family all knew. Colleagues were on the receiving end of feeble attempts at witnessing. Some weeks later he was baptised. After a few more he was making enquiries about being a missionary. He was a changed man.

Nearly nine months later he listened at an adult Sunday School class while people talked about their faith. One woman shared her view. 'The way I understand it is that somehow, while Jesus was hanging on the cross, God laid all our sins on Jesus, so that the penalty we should have had for doing wrong was taken by him instead.'

It was another bolt from the blue for the young man. 'Of course . . .!' he said inwardly, as all sorts of thoughts suddenly slotted into place. It was as if he'd found the key piece for his jigsaw of spiritual truth, and every other piece fitted around it. At that moment and for the first time he began to grasp the doctrine that eventually he heard called the atonement. That day he took a giant step forward in his spiritual understanding.

Date the conversion

For the majority of evangelicals, what the young man heard in that adult group was the gospel. What blazed into his mind late at night nine months earlier was not. Back then he'd believed a man called Jesus had lived, that he'd set an example of godliness, and that he'd made a remarkable sacrifice of his life rather than back away from what he'd taught as the truth. Accurate though that was, as the sum total of belief it fell far short of the core of doctrine a Christian should know. Many a humanist or devotee of another faith would believe as much as he did about Jesus.

So, when did that young man become a Christian? There were two crucial moments for him. The first came during his night of searching. That was the start of a new life, but his understanding was woefully deficient. The second was when he heard the atonement explained, when suddenly the gospel message made real sense to him. Which was his conversion? If he had died after the first experience but before the second, where would he have spent his eternity?

If I'd been a counsellor at an evangelistic event, and he'd come forward with the beliefs he had initially, would I have assured him his faith was already adequate? Never. I'd have reckoned he ought to know much more, and I'd have taken him through a list of important basic truths:

- God loves him, and has a wonderful plan for his life, but he has failed God by not living as God wants
- his way to get right with God is through Jesus, God's

Son, who was sent from heaven to earth, lived a perfect
life and died on his behalf, his sin and suffering taken
by Jesus on the cross
- Jesus is alive now, because God raised him from the
dead
- Jesus is in heaven with his Father, but one day will return
to this earth for those who have faith in him

I've been through several counsellor training courses, and
taught some in recent years. Something like that summary
is what I'd have told the young enquirer, for without a reasonable understanding of those points he couldn't possibly
be a Christian. Fundamental to all counsellor training is
that people must reach an adequate comprehension of the
Christian faith.

When he'd accepted those truths, I'd have invited him
to make a commitment in prayer. The first part of that
prayer would have summarised what he'd come to believe,
since his decision for Christ would be because he now knew
those things to be true. Hopefully he'd have got there.

The pre-eminence of doctrine

Different evangelistic programmes each have slightly vary-
ing emphases. But what they all have in common is the
overriding importance of grasping doctrine. None of them
uses the word 'doctrine' of course – far too user-unfriendly.
But that's what it amounts to: a core of key beliefs. Those
who accept those central tenets of the faith are considered
to have become Christians.

That's how it is, not only with evangelistic crusades, but in
the routine of church life. When someone is being prepared
for church membership, what is he asked about? What he
believes. He's expected to have a sufficient understanding
of the things Christians hold to. If he's picked up some
errors along the way, those innocent heresies are corrected

in a confirmation or baptism class. His knowledge is put right. Eventually when he stands before others, and publicly professes that he's a Christian, he knows what that means.

That's all very fine. Or is it? Problems emerge when those who have been told they're Christians because of what they believe conclude, logically, that as long as they go on believing they go on being Christians.

Is belief all that matters?

Fran was an intelligent, attractive young woman, well-liked by other church members. Her understanding of her faith was good. She'd been in the church for some time, a member of a Bible study group, and she'd done training courses on various aspects of Christianity. We were about to ask her to become a Sunday School teacher. Then, unexpected by all of us, Fran left her husband and moved in with Simon, another of our church members. We were stunned. Eventually Fran and Simon met with me. Conversation was far from easy as they made feeble attempts to justify what they'd done. Deep down they knew their actions didn't fit with New Testament standards for marriage and morality.

'But,' they said vehemently, 'we're staying together.'

'So, do you still consider yourselves Christians?' I asked.

'Of course. We haven't changed anything we believe. Why wouldn't we be Christians?'

I told them, and they didn't like it. They were offended at having doubt cast on their Christian standing. They believed; so they were Christians.

And there are others in churches today whose lives consistently and persistently miss the mark, but who are as passionate in asserting that they are Christians. Some have fallen out with fellow church members, and now won't even speak to them. There are young people, and some not so young, not even trying to avoid sex outside marriage.

Books or magazines are read which would have made my mother's hair curl. Drugs are used and abused. Promises are made but readily abandoned. Gossip and slander are spread with enthusiasm. Work ethics are those of the secular marketplace, materialism is worshipped, self-comfort is justified, evangelism is disregarded. Inconvenient biblical commands are set aside.

What these people have in common is that they all accept fully the basic truths of Christianity. There is a God who loves them, a Saviour who died for them, and a heaven they anticipate being in because they believe.

Who are the Christians?

So, we have two categories of people. There are those like the young man with whom we began who don't believe the right things but who live to please Christ. And there are those who believe exactly the right things but whose lives aren't so very different from anyone else's in the world. Which group are the Christians?

For most evangelicals, what matters most is getting your beliefs right. For years – hundreds of years now – we've been told you can't work your way to heaven, buy your way to heaven, or bribe your way to heaven. Ever since the sixteenth-century Reformation reaction rejected Roman rituals and relics, those of an evangelical persuasion have distanced themselves from the view that sacred objects, practices or people could generate spiritual results. And they've said no to the idea that right living – being good enough – can make anyone acceptable to God. Instead, what Christians have stressed is the need for personal, sincere faith. Paul says Abraham was not justified by works but by what he believed, and likewise our justification is through faith (Rom. 4:2–3; 5:1). The Galatians were warned that supplementing their faith by works of the law was to turn to a 'different gospel', for the real message was 'that a man is not justified by observing the law, but by faith in

Jesus Christ' (Gal. 1:6; 2:16). Thus the *sola fide* (faith alone) principle became fundamental. Providing you believed your eternity was assured.

For the best part of the last couple of centuries, the Western mindset has been conditioned by science, and its stress on facts. What is known? What has been proved to carry validity? What can be shown to be true? These things are to be accepted. Christians now think like that too. Hence they have written books to demonstrate the trustworthiness of the Scriptures, the validity of the gospel records, the reliability of the resurrection accounts. As evidence is put before a jury, so the facts are laid out, inviting acceptance. But mental acceptance of the truth of facts is all that the scientific method requires. No one has to feel anything, nor necessarily do anything as a consequence. (Recognising a law of gravity doesn't mean I have to be committed to it. Most of the time it'll be in my best interests to observe it, but I am perfectly at liberty to 'defy' it if I can do so safely, such as in a jumbo jet.) We've come to think all that matters is determining the truth.

Thus Christians have been told by the Reformation to believe, and told by science to believe facts. And, for many, that's where the full stop comes. You only need to believe. There's little or nothing more. To insist on anything more is to add to the simplicity of salvation by faith.

Since Fran and Simon still believed all they'd ever believed about Christ, they could insist they were still Christians. So do many more, even though their lifestyles are in blatant contrast to what Christ taught.

The insufficiency of believing

What the Bible actually teaches is inconvenient for the Frans and Simons of this world. The Bible rejects the idea that anyone is saved merely by believing the truth. Truth is not devalued but it's never considered sufficient by itself. Faith is certainly required, but so is a life lived for God.

According to the New Testament, real Christianity does not consist only of what you believe. Nor does it consist only of what you do. It consists of doing what you believe.

James stresses that particularly. Faith must be lived out. Not only does he avoid teaching 'justification by faith alone' (a phrase which never appears in the New Testament), he says specifically that justification is not by faith alone. He writes, ' . . . a person is justified by what he does and not by faith alone' (Jas. 2:24). Interestingly, like Paul, he uses Abraham as proof of his point. The patriarch did not merely believe in God's existence and his power. His belief determined what he did, and that was shown clearly when he offered up Isaac on the altar. 'You see that his faith and his actions were working together, and his faith was made complete by what he did' (2:22). Uncompromisingly, James calls it 'useless' to have faith without deeds (2:20).

Worse still, those with nothing more than belief are ranked with demons by James. 'You believe that there is one God. Good! Even the demons believe that – and shudder' (2:19). Of course. The demons know the Old Testament and the New. They know who Christ is and what he has done. They know of God and his love for the world. Actually, they know a whole range of eternal truths lost on even the best educated theologian. In other words, they know the gospel. But even though they know it they're not saved by it. Demons are not Christians because, despite their knowledge, they do not submit to what the gospel teaches. Their lives have not been changed, or, at least not positively changed, because of the gospel's truth. All they do is tremble.

Knowledge alone saves no one.

Believers, but strangers to Jesus

The uselessness of faith alone is not merely James's teaching. It's clearly that of Jesus also. He warned the crowds:

> Not everyone who says to me, 'Lord, Lord,' will enter
> the kingdom of heaven, but only he who does the will
> of my Father who is in heaven. Many will say to me on
> that day, 'Lord, Lord, did we not prophesy in your name,
> and in your name drive out demons and perform many
> miracles?' Then I will tell them plainly, 'I never knew
> you. Away from me, you evildoers!' (Matt. 7:21–3)

These words of Jesus are disturbing. He's talking about
those who called him 'Lord', people who believed the
right things about him and considered themselves to be
Christians. And they'd prophesied, driven out demons
and performed miracles, so they'd also been active with
Christian work. Yet, there had been a flaw. They'd known
the right facts, and busied themselves with good deeds.
But, despite all their apparently correct ideas and spiritual
actions, they hadn't done the will of the Father in heaven.
Thus they remained unrecognised strangers to Jesus. They
would not enter the kingdom of heaven.

Immediately after that, Jesus described the wise man and
the foolish man, the former building on rock and the latter
on sand. As a child in Sunday School, I heard that story
many times, and sang about it even more. I was told the
difference Jesus was illustrating is between the person who
believes in him and the person who doesn't. But it's not.
According to Jesus, the difference is between the person
who hears his words and puts them into practice and the
person who hears his words and does nothing about them.
The crucial factor, he was saying, is not what someone
knows but what someone does.

There's plenty more teaching from Jesus along the same
lines. He told his disciples, 'If anyone would come after
me, he must deny himself and take up his cross daily and
follow me' (Luke 9:23). That was said just after Peter had
declared that Jesus was the Christ, and Jesus had explained
he would die and then rise again. They knew who he was
and what he would do. But Jesus had to tell them that

wasn't enough. Being a disciple required daily self-denial and self-sacrifice.

Later Jesus became concerned about the large numbers who crowded to hear him. This is not known to bother modern preachers, but Jesus was anxious in case people did not understand the full implications of being disciples. 'If anyone comes to me and does not hate his father and mother, his wife and children, his brothers and sisters – yes, even his own life – he cannot be my disciple. And anyone who does not carry his cross and follow me cannot be my disciple' (Luke 14:26–7). Jesus did not mean 'hate' in our modern, emotional sense, but to put in second place. Nevertheless his words are strong – it was a powerful statement about getting right priorities – and no one who heard him could have imagined that if he became a disciple he would get away with anything less than a radical reappraisal of his life's values. Merely accommodating new truths about Jesus would be wholly insufficient.

Even then Jesus wasn't finished. He talked about a man who had to consider whether he was willing to pay the cost of building a tower, and a king who had to think what it would mean to go to war with an enemy. Then he said, 'In the same way, any of you who does not give up everything he has cannot be my disciple' (Luke 14:33). Belief, in the sense of intellectual assent, simply wouldn't do. Jesus required the complete surrender of life. Without that a person could not be his disciple.

No discount on discipleship

Some reached the right beliefs about Jesus but did no more. One was the spiritually anxious man we call the rich young ruler. Mark's gospel says he ran up to Jesus and fell on his knees before him. He must have already had a significant appreciation of the importance of Jesus. ' "Good teacher," he asked, "what must I do to inherit eternal life?" ' (Mark 10:17). Jesus spoke about keeping the commandments, and the man said he'd kept them all. Here was someone who really wanted to go to heaven. So what did Jesus tell him to do? Was it to believe that he was the Messiah and was going to die in his place? Jesus clearly never did counsellor training, for it wasn't. ' "One thing you lack," he said. "Go, sell everything you have and give to the poor, and you will have treasure in heaven. Then come, follow me"' (Mark 10:21). That's all the young ruler had to do, or, at least, that was the first priority. But he wouldn't do it. The man already believed in God and believed quite a bit about Jesus, enough that Jesus never told him to believe anything more. The one thing he lacked was getting rid of his wealth. But he wouldn't part with it; he walked away. Jesus didn't run after him, and say, 'I didn't mean that. Actually, you can have eternal life simply by believing I'm the Son of God.' Most preachers today would have told him that. Jesus didn't. The terms of discipleship were not merely intellectual belief, but belief plus a reoriented lifestyle. The man believed, but he wouldn't accept the consequences of what he believed. He wouldn't sacrifice his wealth in order to follow Jesus; no discount terms of discipleship were available; so he couldn't be a disciple. Jesus let him go.

There were others who aren't remembered so vividly, but whose refusal to live out their faith was just as decisive. John reports that Jesus performed umpteen miracles, but even after all these signs, done before their very eyes, many still would not believe in him. They were nowhere towards becoming Christians (John 12:37). Others, however, had made some spiritual progress: '. . . at the same time many even among the leaders believed in him. But because of the Pharisees they would not confess their faith for fear they would be put out of the synagogue; for they loved praise from men more than praise from God' (John 12:42–3). These were Jewish leaders who saw and heard Jesus, believed him to be the Christ, but kept quiet in order to retain their prominent positions in synagogue life. They now had faith that Jesus was their Messiah. Were they better off for believing that? No, they weren't. They were secret believers. Was that enough? It certainly wasn't. In time judgment would come for them: 'As for the person who hears my words but does not keep them, I do not judge him. For I did not come to judge the world, but to save it. There is a judge for the one who rejects me and does not accept my words; that very word which I spoke will condemn him at the last day' (John 12:47–8). There's no compromise there. They heard Jesus's words but did not 'keep them', they did not put what he said into practice. They preferred the old way, as if they'd heard nothing. So, although secretly they believed all the right things about Jesus, they were as lost as those who never believed at all.

Acceptance despite little knowledge

Therefore, no one in the New Testament is saved on the basis of doctrinal knowledge. In contrast, strangely, many who were saved lacked detailed doctrinal knowledge.

That's true of the converts in Jerusalem on the Day of Pentecost. When Peter preached to the crowd, he used the Old Testament because his hearers were Jews and familiar with it. He quoted verses which showed that God's Messiah would not be left in the grave but raised to life. Now someone had been raised to life. From the dead God had raised Jesus. God had made 'Lord and Christ' the one they had crucified (Acts 2:36). The crowd was stunned. Peter preached some more. They were even more stunned, repented, and some three thousand were baptised the same day.

How much did those three thousand know of Christianity? According to their own description, they were mostly not locals – 'Parthians, Medes and Elamites; residents of Mesopotamia, Judea and Cappadocia, Pontus and Asia, Phrygia and Pamphylia, Egypt and the parts of Libya near Cyrene; visitors from Rome (both Jews and converts to Judaism); Cretans and Arabs' (Acts 2:9–11).

These people were not Jerusalem's core population. They'd come especially for Pentecost, seven weeks after Passover. Probably the vast majority had never heard Jesus, seen his miracles, or been at Calvary. Some may have been told of Jesus, but most made their commitment based on what Peter preached that day.

In terms of Christian doctrine he hadn't told them much. He said God had accredited Jesus of Nazareth with signs and wonders, but they were guilty of crucifying him. They'd put God's Messiah on a cross. The resurrection was proof that Jesus was the Christ, and now they must seek forgiveness for what they'd done, and save themselves from their corrupt generation.

There's nothing untrue about any of that, of course, but by itself it's an incomplete doctrinal summary. In particular, what Peter missed telling them is that Jesus took their sins on himself when he went to the cross. He never explained the atonement. In fact, none of the sermons in the book of Acts ever describes how forgiveness comes. The early preachers of Acts spoke much about repentance and forgiveness, but not one spelled out that Jesus sacrificed himself in our place on the cross. Either they never said it or the writer of Acts never reported it. Whichever, a key evangelical truth, perhaps the essence of the whole gospel, was far from prominent. But thousands upon thousands of the most earnest and committed Christians there have ever been were born again without hearing it explicitly. Their understanding was lacking, but still they got saved.

Thief, apostle, betrayer – which knew the truth and which were saved?

If we pick three New Testament characters – the dying thief, the apostle Paul and Judas Iscariot – only one had a real grasp of Christianity. And he was the one who wasn't saved.

The first of these three could be described as about the

most 'ignorant' of all converts, the thief who hung on a cross, sharing Calvary with Jesus. His fellow criminal insulted Jesus, but this man rebuked him. ' "Don't you fear God," he said, "since you are under the same sentence? We are punished justly, for we are getting what our deeds deserve. But this man has done nothing wrong." Then he said, "Jesus, remember me when you come into your kingdom" ' (Luke 23:40–2).

And that was all he said. What kind of Christian confession was that? Where was his prayer of commitment? In particular, how much doctrine did he know? What of atonement, justification, sanctification? Of these 'technical' details he knew little and cared less. Perhaps he had been taught as a child about the Messiah. But whatever he'd learned would have hindered rather than helped, since Jesus did not fit the traditional Jewish concept of an all-conquering Messiah, especially when he hung on the cross. At best the man's comprehension of Christian doctrine was that Jesus claimed to be the Christ (the first criminal had mentioned that), that Jesus was a good man who ought not to be crucified, and that somehow Jesus could grant him a place in his kingdom. That was it. But it was enough. 'Jesus answered him, "I tell you the truth, today you will be with me in paradise" ' (v.42). His knowledge was rudimentary, but he trusted his life to Jesus. That's what mattered, and Jesus accepted him.

Character number two is a very different kind of person. Paul, the Pharisee, probably had an immense theological grasp. But what he knew of Jesus and his message drove him to hunt down Christians and put them to death. It did not make him one of them. Then he set out for Damascus, and was converted on the journey. What caused his conversion? Did some brave Christian travel with him and explain the gospel's deeper truths? No one was that brave. Did Paul turn over in his mind all he'd heard Stephen or other Christians preach, and suddenly see the rightness of it? There's no record of that. What is recorded is a sudden light flashing round Paul, a collapse to the ground, and the voice of Jesus speaking to him. Paul was met by Jesus. The Jesus he had been persecuting was clearly alive. And that changed his life. For three days Paul was blind. Then Ananias came, and his sight was restored. Both the risen Christ and Ananias spoke to Paul, but in none of the three accounts in Acts of Paul's conversion (Acts 9:1–19; 22:3–16; 26:9–18) is there any mention of Paul having the gospel explained more clearly to him. What made the difference – what led to his conversion – was meeting Christ.

The third character is unlike either of the first two. Of the three, Judas is the one with the vast knowledge of Jesus. One of the Twelve, he'd spent two or three years travelling the road with him. Day in, day out he'd heard his teaching and watched what he did. He was there when Peter declared to Jesus, 'You are the Christ, the Son of the living God' (Matt. 16:16). Following that confession Jesus had taught the disciples 'that he must go to Jerusalem and suffer many things at the hands of the elders, chief priests and teachers of the law, and that he must be killed and on the third day be raised to life' (Matt. 16:21). Judas knew these things on the best authority, Jesus himself. And there was more, much more. Judas' mastery of Jesus's teaching was second to none. And every word he heard from Jesus he saw validated by a life of purity and power. Christ's goodness – his holiness, his godliness – was before Judas' eyes daily. So was his divine authority, demonstrated by walking on water, healing the sick, casting out demons, and even raising the dead. When these miracles were happening Judas was watching at close quarters. And he believed. Peter was speaking on behalf of every one of the Twelve, including Judas, when he said to Jesus, 'You have the words of eternal life. We believe and know that you are the Holy One of God' (John 6:68–9). And specifically of Judas, Peter could say later, 'he was one of our number and shared in this ministry' (Acts 1:17).

Did all this make Judas a Christian? Far from it. Instead

of Christ being in Judas, the New Testament twice says
Satan entered into him (Luke 22:3; John 13:27). He's called
a 'betrayer' (Mark 14:44) and a 'traitor' (Luke 6:16). Jesus's
own verdict on him was that he was a 'devil' (John 6:70).

Is he in heaven now? That would hardly fit with Jesus's
statement that it would have been better for Judas if he had
never been born (Matt. 26:24). Nor is heaven the eternal
destination which the early Christians had in mind when,
in prayer, they referred to Judas leaving 'to go where he
belongs' (Acts 1:25). In fact, Jesus sums up Judas' fate in
his prayer, 'None has been lost except the one doomed to
destruction . . .' (John 17:12).

So Judas knew it all and saw it all. The dying thief hardly
knew or saw anything, and whatever knowledge Paul had
turned him against Christianity. Yet, while Judas headed
for what older versions called perdition, the thief and Paul
headed for paradise. What makes someone a Christian is
not merely knowledge of the gospel.

Two-sided coin

According to the Bible, conversion involves both new
knowledge and new lifestyle. Knowledge alone won't
do. Those who claim they love Jesus must live that
out. 'If you love me, you will obey what I command,'
said Jesus (John 14:15). And he said, '. . . every good
tree bears good fruit, but a bad tree bears bad fruit.
Thus, by their fruit you will recognise them' (Matt. 7:17,
20). What people do is evidence of what they believe.
Equally, a good lifestyle without knowing Jesus won't do
either. At Ephesus Paul found 'disciples' who had already
committed themselves to God through John's baptism.
That wasn't enough. 'Paul said, "John's baptism was a
baptism of repentance. He told the people to believe in
the one coming after him, that is, in Jesus." On hearing
this, they were baptised into the name of the Lord Jesus'
(Acts 19:4–5).

Salvation is not a single-sided coin. The New Testament never teaches that someone can be saved by faith without works, nor does it teach that someone can be saved by works without faith. Either without the other falls short of biblical conversion.

Plenty of evangelicals are clear enough that they're relying on their faith and not their works. Not so many give full value to the other side of the salvation coin.

Antinomianism was around as a heresy from early centuries of the Church's life. Put simply, people said they were no longer under law but under grace, so what they did was of no consequence as long as they believed. Orthodox Christians have never accepted that. But modern-day evangelicals are in danger of a creeping antinomianism. They shrug their shoulders, and say, 'I know I should be better, but since I believe the gospel God will save me anyway. What I'm like doesn't matter.'

It does. It matters very much since Jesus has said it is impossible to be a Christian without denying self, carrying the cross and following him. A life of discipleship is part of the deal. Christianity is not merely believing the truth about Jesus. It's living it out.

This chapter began with the story of a young man whose theology was faulty but who gave his life to Christ nevertheless. Did he become a Christian back then? I hope so. That was me.

What I knew made me want to commit myself to Jesus. My ideas were flawed and inadequate, but if heaven is reserved for those with perfect theology, it won't suffer from overcrowding. I believed enough about Jesus to know I needed to trust only in him for salvation, and that I ought to make him my Lord in every detail of life.

There was lots to learn. I'm thankful I've been in a position to study it. Many don't have that opportunity, or aren't able to grasp the niceties of the faith. But

Jesus takes anyone who knows sufficient of his love and goodness that they're willing to become his disciple. Thank God that's what it's about. Thank God it doesn't depend on our cleverness or comprehension.

3

To be more effective as Christians we need more prayer

I couldn't sleep. Though my body longed for rest, my mind was in overdrive. Restless thoughts raced here and there, soaring to the sublime and plummeting to the ridiculous. Mostly the ridiculous had the edge. I wondered if I would ever win the fight against weeds in my garden, and worried why I kept slicing my tee-shots when I attempted to play golf. 'I should be concerned about a lost world,' I chided myself.

In the distance I heard the town clock strike one. For a brief moment my eyes rested. Then again I was awake. Nothing could convince my brain to let me sleep.

Time dragged, every minute seeming endless. I reckoned it must be near two o'clock. Sure enough, from the town square I heard the deep gong of the clock. I waited for the second strike. Suddenly I wasn't alone. There was a figure in my room, a man whose presence somehow lit the room so I could see him clearly. Terror gripped my mind and body. I screamed but no sound emerged.

He spoke. 'Be at peace.'

At peace? I was nearly at the mortuary.

'You are concerned for this lost world . . .'

Well, I was, though I was also worried about my weeds and slicing my golf shots. It seemed tactful to nod quietly.

'I will show you what God's people are doing for the lost.

Come with me.' It didn't sound like an invitation I could refuse. Lamely I nodded again.

In an instant we were out of my bedroom, engulfed in the darkness of the night, but immediately emerging into the brightness of a church service. My eyes took a moment to focus. When they did, I was startled by the familiarity of the scene. It was my own church, and one of our services. My escort and I were there yet not there. Somehow we could absorb the whole service in a moment of time.

'Reasonable singing . . .' I said positively, looking to my companion for approval.

'Listen to what is being preached,' he replied.

I focused on the preacher, and drew in my breath sharply. It was me! This was not going to be a good experience. I hated listening to my own sermons; every wrong word or voice inflection or hesitation was torture. Yet – hold on – I remembered this sermon. It was a good one! Lots of people had thanked me afterwards, and often quoted later what I'd said. It was based on Jesus's command to the disciples just before he left them. 'Do not leave Jerusalem, but wait for the gift my Father promised, which you have heard me speak about. For John baptised with water, but in a few days you will be baptised with the Holy Spirit. You will receive power when the Holy Spirit comes on you; and you will be my witnesses in Jerusalem, and in all Judea and Samaria, and to the ends of the earth' (Acts 1:4–5, 8). I watched and heard myself preaching the passage with passion. Key phrases jumped into my mind.

Jesus wouldn't let them witness without power. Sure, Jerusalem had to be won, and so did Judea, Samaria and the ends of the earth. But he commanded them not to go, not until they had power . . .

What we need too is more power from God. Without that our witness is doomed to failure. There's no point in going to your neighbour, or your colleague, and no point in this church organising any evangelism, if we don't have power. But with power, we'll see not ones or twos coming to Christ, but

*thousands, just like the apostles did when they were filled with
power at Pentecost. Seek more of God and God's strength. If
we're going to be more effective as Christians we must wait
for the Father's gift. More than anything, we need to come
before our Father – take time to really pray – and find more
of his power.*

Not bad, I thought. I turned to my companion for
approval, but already the church service was receding
quickly. There was a flash of darkness, and then a new
scene unfolded before me.

It was our church's crash course in evangelism. A smug
grin grew on my face. I remembered this meeting. 'No one
will come' – so had predicted the church gurus who thought
they had all wisdom. But plenty had, a hundred who wanted
to know how to pass on their faith.

The programme for the night scrolled past my eyes:
making contacts; the summary of the gospel; sharing your
testimony; memorising key texts; leading someone to Christ;
getting the convert started on follow-up. What an evening it
had been, a two-hour package of everything the potential
witness needed to know.

I heard myself drawing the evening to a close. *You've
been given the resources now, and there are plenty out there
who need Christ. This time next week, I'd like you in one
of two places. Either be back here ready to go round the
doors in our neighbourhood to put into practice what you've
learned tonight. Or be through in our other hall to pray for
those who do the visiting. Together we can do the task:
front-line troops battling for the gospel on the doorstep,
and support troops pleading with God so that their battle
is effective.*

'Do you remember the following week?' my companion
asked.

'Every one of them came back,' I said with only the
mildest hint of pride.

'And how many went out to share their faith and how
many prayed?'

Pride evaporated. 'I think about five went witnessing, and ninety-five stayed to pray.'

He nodded and said nothing.

'Biggest attendance ever at a prayer meeting . . .' I tried to plead, but my pitiful words were lost in the whirl of another move.

A split second later we were at our church weekend conference. The big-name speaker was laying forth, and everyone seemed to be paying him rapt attention. Lots were even taking notes. I remembered wondering why they never did that when I spoke. Overall, though, I'd been glad so many had turned up. When you book someone two years ahead, and fly him the length of the country, you put pride away and hope your people bother to come. They'd drunk in every word he said.

The part of our programme I'd been brought to now was the Saturday evening anything-may-happen-tonight meeting. 'Find your spiritual gift' was the practical title we'd given it. That had struck a chord with many. They knew they were supposed to have spiritual gifts, but weren't sure what gifts they did or didn't have. This conference session was especially for them.

Again I seemed to be able to grasp the whole meeting in an instant. I sensed their expectancy, warmed to the worship and felt inspired by the speaker. Somehow, as if my companion wanted it, my mind focused on one part of his talk.

It was about Ephesians 4:11, 'It was he who gave some to be apostles, some to be prophets, some to be evangelists, and some to be pastors and teachers'. *Is everyone an apostle?* he was asking. *Is everyone a prophet? Is everyone an evangelist, or a pastor/teacher? You're not all any of these things. God has made each of you differently and given you unique gifts. Many want the gifts they see in others, and don't like the gifts they've been given. That's the road to spiritual poverty. Don't think you can steal someone else's gift; you'll bear no fruit trying to do what you're not gifted for. And if you neglect the gift you have, the church misses out on God's work through you.*

On he went, going through each of these role-gifts. As if it was underlined, I heard him say, *Not everyone has been made an evangelist – probably only ten per cent have a real gift of evangelism. But if you're part of the other ninety per cent, you can be a prayer warrior for the evangelists. Prayer changes things. By prayer you can equip the evangelists for the work to which they're called and you're not.*

I was moved as I sensed the power of those words, and I remembered how the whole weekend had helped so many. They'd been released from long-held guilt about things they didn't feel able to do. Even fewer than usual had helped distribute Easter cards to local homes three weeks later. In fact, so few had volunteered, the organiser had been forced to cut back on the number of cards the church could distribute. But at least those which were given out had gone surrounded by the prayers of more people than ever before.

The scene retreated, a moment of darkness, and then bright sunlight. A wall of heat, colour and noise hit me. I peered through half-shut eyes, trying to work out where I was. Children scampered to and fro, black-skinned youngsters with flashing smiles, clothed in little other than torn shorts and dirty tee shirts. I saw huts scattered across a compound of baked earth. Women gutted fish ready for cooking; men sat in the shade of a tree.

'I recognise this!' I shouted incredulously to my escort. 'This is Africa, and I was in this village when I visited Barbara, one of our church's missionaries.'

As if on cue, there she was, walking through the compound, stopping at hut after hut to talk. I understood nothing she said, for she was using the tribal language. But I guessed the gist of part of it, for every conversation started with lengthy greeting rituals which had to be gone through before it was possible to speak about anything else.

Barbara knows these people so well, I thought. I watched

her hold a newborn baby, cradle it gently, tactfully easing back the woollen bonnet which looked pretty but was far too warm for this climate. She walked on, intercepted by an old woman who shuffled along on her knees. Dark bracelets covered the woman's arms, and charms hung from her neck. I'd met her – the stories of her spirit powers had made me shiver. Barbara played with little children, talked with a young man coming home from the fields, sat with a sick grandmother for whom medicine to make her better was more than her family could pay.

As I looked on, thoughts which I'd suppressed pushed to the surface. I saw how alone she was and how hopeless her task. For fifteen years she'd visited these people, poured her love into them, told them and retold them the gospel. What did she have to show for all that in this village? One man had believed, but when his family made life too difficult for him, he'd gone back to his native religion. And that was it. There was no one else. Sure there were other contacts in other places, and Barbara hoped some of them might stick with believing in Christ, but really there was so little for so much effort and sacrifice.

'We know it's hard, and back home we really pray for Barbara,' I said.

My companion didn't respond. Instead, it seemed he caused other memories to resurface, things Barbara had told me. *If only there were more of us here sharing the gospel. I can get to this village only once a week now. There are hundreds of these villages in just this area, and most know nothing of Christ. The people haven't heard the gospel and rejected it; hardly any of them have ever heard it. There are millions in this country, and only a handful of us to reach them. Is there no one else who can come?*

I'd done my best when I'd got home. I'd shown pictures of the village, told the stories of some of the people, and passed on Barbara's plea. 'We must pray more for Barbara and that country,' several had said. And they had. For a long time their needs were at the top of the church's prayer agenda.

No one else went to work in that part of Africa though. There were still just Barbara and a handful of missionaries for millions of people.

I sighed, but then we took off yet again. If the last scene was bright, this one was dazzling. A huge ball of light met my eyes, so intense I couldn't look straight at it. I squinted through screwed-up eyelids, and gradually became aware of a vast crowd, people of all ages, all nations, all types. The air felt strange, and so did the sounds, as if not from this world. 'They're not from your world,' said my companion, and I realised he knew my thoughts. 'This is the place of judgment.'

As I looked on, I saw a division take place among the people. A few, very few, were taken to one side. The rest, a great throng, silent and submissive, were moved the other way. Like the separation of the sheep and the goats, I told myself. Sadly I knew which were the goats. 'Eternal loss . . .? Hell . . .? For all these . . .?'

There was a nod from the figure beside me.

As the crowd melted away, my eyes fixed on a few among these lost ones. 'My neighbours! And there's my cousin and his wife! And the people who live just down the road from our church, and Doug who partners me in golf matches. The folk who work in the shop on the corner. And Africans – hundreds, thousands, must be millions – exactly the people Barbara was trying to reach.'

Even as I spoke the scene dimmed. A millisecond of darkness was replaced by familiar surroundings. It was my bedroom, and I was sitting up in bed staring awkwardly at the companion I now presumed to be an angelic taxi man.

'So many lost,' he said quietly. 'People loved by God. People his Son died for.'

The words were stated as truths, not accusations, but I felt I had to say something. 'We prayed for them – particularly those I noticed in the crowd. Not just once. Over and over we prayed – for our families, our neighbours, the people near our church, our contacts, our city, and for those in other lands. We really prayed for them.'

'You said you were concerned for the lost, and I have shown you what you are doing for the lost. Judge for yourself if your prayers are enough.'

His words hung in the air. Then he was gone and it was as if he was never there. In the distance I heard a single strike from the town clock. I looked at my watch. It was two o'clock. Whatever had happened – five visits – had been between the first and second strikes of the clock.

I lay back on my bed, and tried to make sense of it all. Perhaps that was impossible, but, as the night wore on, this much I grew to know: I wouldn't be telling my people again that to be more effective as Christians all they needed was more prayer.

Now, everything about those flying visits is a product of imagination, not experience. The restless nights are real enough, but only in my mind have I seen these different scenes. Yet I fear their truth. While we bow our heads interceding for those who don't know Christ, more and more of them are drifting into a lost eternity. Can that be right?

'More prayer, pastor'

These days people are not shy about giving advice to pastors. Of all the things I'm told the most common is that we don't have enough prayer. 'God wants us to pray more,' say many. 'We need more time on our knees if we're to achieve anything as Christians.' And the revivalists add, 'If we would only stop all our activities and get back to seeking God, then real blessings would start to fall. Not a tiny trickle but a major downpour.'

A whole catalogue of spiritual giants from the past point to prayer as the key to effectiveness for Christian work. For example, here's A.T. Pierson: 'From the Day of Pentecost, there has not been one great spiritual awakening in any land which has not begun in a union of prayer, though only among two or three; no such outward, upward movement has continued after such prayer meetings have declined' (A.T. Pierson, quoted by A. Wallis in *In the Day of Thy Power* [Christian Literature Crusade, 1956], p. 112).

Uncompromising statements like that are made so often and with such apparent authority, no one dares to argue. Thus, when we don't see hordes of people coming to Christ, it must be because of a lack of prayer. The Bible warns us of that danger: 'You do not have, because you do not ask God' (Jas. 4:2).

In fact, the Bible seems to regard prayer as the precondition for any great movement of God. 'If my people, who are called by my name, will humble themselves and pray and seek my face and turn from their wicked ways, then will I hear from heaven and will forgive their sin and will heal their land' (2 Chr. 7:14).

'*If* my people . . . will pray . . . *then* will I hear from heaven . . . and will heal their land,' says God. Unless we pray – until we pray – our land will remain 'unhealed'. It'll be spiritually sick. We can witness until we're blue in the face, but we'll see no significant results.

Perhaps we have to win a battle in the heavenlies before we can see victory on earth. Paul warned: 'For our struggle is not against flesh and blood, but against the rulers, against the authorities, against the powers of this dark world and against the spiritual forces of evil in the heavenly realms' (Eph. 6:12). Neither human effort nor human cleverness can defeat spiritual powers; only spiritual weapons can do that, and prayer heads the armaments list.

A classic example of that in practice comes with King Jehoshaphat of Judah. A three-nation alliance of Moabites, Ammonites and Meunites made war on him. Jehoshaphat's forces were massively outnumbered, and it looked like the nation would be ravaged. What did Jehoshaphat do? 'Alarmed, Jehoshaphat resolved to enquire of the LORD, and he proclaimed a fast for all Judah. The people of

Judah came together to seek help from the LORD; indeed, they came from every town in Judah to seek him' (2 Chr. 20:3–4). So they prayed. And when they prayed God spoke to them through one of the prophets:

> This is what the LORD says to you: 'Do not be afraid or discouraged because of this vast army. For the battle is not yours, but God's. You will not have to fight this battle. Take up your positions; stand firm and see the deliverance the LORD will give you, O Judah and Jerusalem. Do not be afraid; do not be discouraged. Go out to face them tomorrow, and the LORD will be with you.' (20:15, 17)

They took God seriously. Next day Jehoshaphat put the singers – his worship group – at the head of the army. When they began to praise God, God set ambushes for their enemies who began to fight among themselves. The outcome was dramatic: 'When the men of Judah came to the place that overlooks the desert and looked towards the vast army, they saw only dead bodies lying on the ground; no-one had escaped' (20:24). Jehoshaphat and his army witnessed the utter defeat of the invaders without having to strike a blow. They prayed, and the war was won.

It's so easy like that. If we would bother to wait on God in prayer, so much of our effort and striving for success – which usually doesn't get us far – would be unnecessary.

Shutting God out

Maybe our problem is pride. We claim we trust God, but actually we prefer to be in control ourselves. We daren't let go; we're not sure God would do what we want or do it the way we want. Yes, we pray – our evangelicalism requires it – but there's no real handing over of situations to God. Though we'd never come out with it, in effect we say, 'I don't need the Lord.'

Unsurprisingly, then, we have little power and see little of God at work. Jesus put it bluntly: 'Apart from me you can do nothing' (John 15:5). When we press ahead with our best-thought-out strategies then all we have is that – our best ideas. They don't save people. They don't have the power to work miracles. To serve prayerlessly is pride, a pride which says 'I can do it' and shuts God out. But when we put our plans aside and engage in real prayer we hand the work over to God. He does save people and he does have miracle-working power. God is freed to go to work, and we can stand back in awe and praise. Humility abandons self-effort. Humility seeks God in prayer and gives him the space to do his work in his way.

The point is obvious. If we are to be more effective as Christians we need more prayer.

At times that's probably right. But not always. The truth can be the opposite of that. To be more effective as Christians there should be less prayer.

When prayer is sin

At the least charitable there are evangelicals who prefer to pray than work, who prefer the comparative safety of bowing their heads and talking to God rather than risking embarrassment or opposition by talking to the world. They're lazy or scared, or both. A little more charitably, there are evangelicals who, if they came from a different tradition, would happily be monks or nuns and consider it their calling to be on near-permanent retreat to pray for lost humanity.

For different reasons, these people claim the priority of prayer, their need to live close to God if they are to be used by him, and that their prayers show trust in God rather than themselves. It sounds so spiritual. But it's not spiritual if they're praying when God has called them to work. Too much of a good thing makes it a bad thing.

through the clouds and blasting earth with his message. He had chosen to speak to people through people. So he told those who believed to put the gospel before those who didn't yet believe: 'you will be my witnesses in Jerusalem, and in all Judea and Samaria, and to the ends of the earth' (Acts 1:8). It was their work to present the gospel, their work to bring others to faith, their work to make them into disciples. Does an employee get instructions from his boss and later ask the boss to do the very things he was instructed to do? Of course not. No one but God could do the miracle of creating saving faith, but the fundamental task of presenting Christ to lost people was theirs. Suppose the work got dangerous? Even then they couldn't hand the commission back to God and tell him to handle it himself. Whatever it took, this was *their* calling. So they didn't pray for people to be saved; they prayed for boldness to keep witnessing no matter how difficult or costly it became. That way people would hear of Jesus, and God could give the gift of new life to all who had faith.

Effectiveness is not a product of goodness

What about the idea that God can't use you unless you are living close to him? As we trust our deepest secrets or most important work to our closest friends, so those who have come nearest to God will surely be the ones to hear his voice and receive his power, and thus be most effective. Since we relate to him more intimately in prayer than any other way, prayer becomes the key to ever-greater usefulness for God.

That's good logic, but not good theology.

First, it makes a common human assumption that good things come to those who are good. We're brainwashed from birth with that idea – 'Tidy your room and I'll read you a story' – and we carry that way of thinking into spiritual matters without realising we're doing it. So, God will use us only if we've kept enough of his laws and, in particular, only if we've spent enough time in prayer to him.

Unfortunately, 'enough' by God's definition is perfection, which doesn't leave any of us placed too well. Fortunately, doing 'enough' of anything is not the basis of God's fellowship with us, God's empowering of us, or God's willingness to use us. Rather, just as God accepts us initially on the basis of his grace – his decision to be merciful – and not on the basis of our goodness, so God continues to relate to us that way. There's no score of merit that any of us must achieve before God wants us or before he can do things through us. We don't have to reach a target of being at least a three-star prayer warrior before we can be effective witnesses. And becoming a four-star 'pray-er' won't make us better witnesses. We cannot earn God's power.

Second, there are countless biblical examples of people not living close to God who were nevertheless greatly used by him. Abraham abandoned God's plan that he should have a child with Sarah and instead made his wife's maid pregnant. Yet God didn't give up on him, and in her old age Sarah finally conceived and Isaac was born. David also made the wrong woman pregnant, and then added to his crime by organising the contract killing of her husband. Yet he was still Israel's greatest king. All the apostles, and Peter especially, swore they would never run out on Jesus but would be loyal even to death. What happened? When arrest came, every one of them deserted and Peter blatantly denied ever knowing Jesus. Yet these were the men on whom God sent his Holy Spirit at Pentecost, men who went on to do amazing miracles for him. Weak failures are still accepted and used by God.

Perhaps the most dramatic example is Jonah. His story opens with God giving him a specific and well-understood command to preach to Nineveh. Jonah blatantly refused. Nineveh was the home of his worst enemies, and he didn't want God showing them mercy. He took a ship in the opposite direction but was thrown overboard to quell a storm, swallowed by a large fish, and eventually vomited up on land. Jonah realised God wasn't taking 'no' for an answer. Reluctantly he went to Nineveh, walked some distance into the city, and preached his message: 'Forty more days and Nineveh will be overturned' (Jonah 3:4). That was hardly the greatest presentation of the gospel there's ever been. Perhaps Jonah hoped no one would pay any attention. He was wrong. Every one of the Ninevites took him seriously. They believed God had spoken through him, began to fast, dressed in sackcloth, gave up their evil ways, and called on God for mercy. God saw their response, set aside his judgment and forgave them. There were at least one hundred and twenty thousand people in Nineveh, so their repentance may well mark the greatest ever single response to a sermon.

Despite Jonah's initial rebellion, God had used him to bring about a wonderful miracle of changed lives. He ought to have been glad. He was far from it: 'Jonah was greatly displeased and became angry' (Jonah 4:1). The story ends with Jonah thoroughly out of sorts with God. In fact he was like that all the way through. He disagreed with God at the start, and never changed his mind. So, here was a man whose life was wrong with God, yet he was used to bring revival to a whole city. Jonah is one of many through whom God did a great work even though his life was spiritually weak.

It's bad theology to say that effective Christian work depends on personal spirituality, whether that spirituality is measured by a great prayer life or anything else. God deals with us on the basis of grace, not on the basis of a pass mark in spiritual exercises. More or less prayer does not automatically make us more or less usable by God.

Prayer does not equal trust

Surely prayerlessness is pride, as if we think we don't need God? So, when Jesus told his disciples that without him they could do nothing, he was teaching against self-reliance.

Their skills and power were nothing like enough to do the work of God; they needed to trust him.

Yes, they needed to trust him, and Jesus's words support that truth. But what they don't support is the assumption that you can measure trust in God by the amount of time spent in prayer.

If I talk to a second-hand-car salesman, does it mean I trust him? If I forget to phone my father, does it mean I don't trust him? A high or low point on a scale of communication does not equate directly with a high or low point on a scale of trust. There are some who spend hours in prayer, but they still don't really trust God. There are some who spend little time in head-bowed formal prayer; but have a great trust in God. What matters is God-reliance, not the amount of prayer.

Sometimes, of course, prayer is the way of declaring that reliance.

So it was with Jehoshaphat. As his enemies descended on him, he prayed: 'O our God, will you not judge them? For we have no power to face this vast army that is attacking us. We do not know what to do, but our eyes are upon you' (2 Chr. 20:12). Jehoshaphat's last few words are the key. The future of God's people was at stake, and they were looking to God for rescue. They had complete trust. Jehoshaphat's prayer stated it, and marching out next morning armed with praises proved it.

So it was in a different way with God's promise to Solomon, that if the nation prayed and sought God's face, he would hear and heal the land. Those words don't show the priority of prayer. They show the need to surrender lives to God, and thus how to end God's judgment on the land.

When I shut up the heavens so that there is no rain, or command locusts to devour the land or send a plague among my people, if my people, who are called by my name, will humble themselves and pray and seek my face of all this. There again was that great but terrible divide on the day of judgment. This time, though, while many still went away to a lost eternity, a great number remained to be welcomed into the Father's kingdom. Among them were those I had seen at the beginning of this dream so intent on prayer. But not just them. Beside them were also some of their families, some who lived in the street near the church building, some who had been visited in their homes, some who had been unmarried mothers, some rescued from addiction, some who had died from AIDS. All these together entering glory!

The Christians had prayed for them, yet not only prayed for them but reached out the hand of God to them. Never before had they been so effective as Christians.

4

Only real sins matter

Coming to church should help people avoid sin, but it seems attendance at our services encourages our members into sin. Most arrive by car, but, because we're near the city centre in a building erected a hundred years ago, we have no car park. That isn't much of a difficulty on Sundays, for nearby streets have little traffic and there are plenty of places to park. But some people are lazy and many are late, so they leave their cars as near as they can to the church building. Often that means they leave them where they're not supposed to. Double yellow lines decorate the edges of the street, with little notices pinned nearby to communicate that parking there is prohibited at any time.

We tell the people to find other parking places. What they're doing is against the law, and it's not a good witness to those who live nearby who see church people not bothering to keep to the rules. We're not asking much of our people. At most they'll have a five-minute walk. For a week or two there's a difference, until the first Sunday when it's raining and then they're back to old habits. There's no dispute about the fact that illegal parking is wrong. But they keep doing it. Why? Because they think parking where you're not supposed to doesn't *really* matter. And the traffic wardens don't work on Sundays so they won't get a parking ticket. Authority without accountability is meaningless.

My church members have defined illegal parking as being less than a real sin. Evangelicals in general seem as skilled as weren't in a position to commit, but wished they could. Give most Christians the chance to have serious money and they'll soon find a way of dealing with their scruples.

Hooked on soaps

If you want to be in a minority of one in defining a sin, try preaching that Christians ought not to watch TV soap operas. I've found that ranks in the popularity stakes alongside telling Baptists to sprinkle babies, Presbyterians to elect bishops, Anglicans to burn prayer books, and Catholics to go twice as often to confession. Just not on. I could condemn murder and rape, adultery and lying, or the youth club for leaving the church hall in a mess, but I must not say anything bad about the soaps.

I'd thought the point was reasonable when I preached on Romans 12:2. Paul commands Christians to have renewed minds, minds which are not conformed to the pattern of this world. If 'garbage in, garbage out' is a self-evident truth, it's impossible, I said, to have healthily renewed minds if we give them unhealthy diets. TV soaps major on gossip, lust, hate and violence. Make that our daily input, and that's how we'll think.

When I preach these things my congregation are unimpressed. As they leave after the service, some openly disagree. They tell me they're 'keeping in touch with real life', which makes me wonder how unreal their lives are normally. Most just smile indulgently at me. 'Shame Alistair has these hang-ups,' they probably think. Whatever I say they've no intention of changing their viewing habits.

Many are completely hooked. They could not miss an episode. The only reason their mid-evening programmes don't stop them coming to church meetings is because they have video recorders, and they go home later and catch up. A clash of two soaps and a church event constitutes a major crisis. But they seem to know what everyone else watches, and they're soon on the phone negotiating. 'If you video that programme, I'll video the other one, and we can swap tapes tomorrow.' One fellow nearly missed out when he accepted an invitation to spend the evening with friends. His programme is broadcast at seven o'clock and he wouldn't be home for it. The problem was that his soap is on the radio, and he doesn't have the facilities to time a radio recording. But he solved it. When 7 p.m. came he asked his hosts if they would tune in their radio so he could hear his programme. They obliged, and for twenty minutes all of them sat staring at the wall while he caught up with the happenings in his favourite fictional village. That's dedication. Or addiction.

Christians don't think that's wrong. But they turn up for counselling, telling me they can't get rid of evil thoughts, or can't forgive those who hurt them, or can't control their behaviour, or can't find time for Bible study or prayer. I preach some more about how we should guard our minds, and be careful what we listen to or watch on TV. And they argue with me or smile at me again. A few take heed; most don't. After all, watching TV – no matter what's on – can never be a real sin, not one that counts.

Climbing the career ladder

Chasing a career is another sin that isn't a sin, according to most evangelicals. The average length of time someone is a member of our church is three years. That's not because they get fed up with us and move to another congregation. It's because most are in their twenties and thirties, on the early or mid rungs of their career ladders, and they want to go higher. So either by their choice or their employers' they relocate. We have more farewell parties than any other kind of social event.

The continual mobility of these people has major effects.

direction. After all, look at the experience he's had in so many previous churches. Precisely. But none of this is sin, or, at least no one usually says it is.

Company growth, no matter the price

Nor is it sin, apparently, when an employer causes hardships for the sake of his business.

The Christian boss sits in church on Sunday, listening to a moving sermon on loving his neighbour or the importance of marriage. Next day he is shown a financial analysis which suggests that reorganisation will help his business. Decisive leader that he is, he acts. He makes two long-serving employees redundant, saving on their wages now and avoiding a large contribution to their eventual pension. And he closes a branch office, dismissing two more staff and recalling another to head office. All this will boost company profits by 0.02 per cent.

What, though, of the price to those involved? Redundancy for those past age fifty-five probably means never working again, with long-term financial hardship. In a recessionary economy, even younger people will struggle to get new employment. The relocated staff member is better off, it seems, but what if yet another move is the final pressure on a shaky marriage and it breaks, destroying a family unit? The previous day's sermon is forgotten by the company boss. Good entrepreneurs never lose sight of their goal: maximise profits. They don't compromise that goal by allowing their decisions to be affected by the personal well-being of their staff. Martin is needed in London? Move him to London. Six months later, Martin is needed back in Aberdeen? Move him back to Aberdeen. Next stop Houston, Texas. Or there's a chance to exploit a competitor's weakness, steal his business, drive him into bankruptcy and put him out of business? Take it. Five hundred will be thrown out of work, but take it. Who condemns a boss for prioritising his company's earnings?

As long as he breaks no laws, tells no lies, and turns in a healthy balance sheet, he's doing his job well. Some have suffered along the way, but others now work for an even more secure firm. The trail of devastation in the lives of those who were moved or sacked is the price worth paying for progress. That infinitesimal gain in the balance sheet *is* progress, isn't it? Who's calling it sin?

The wrong sacrifice

Likewise, who's willing to call it sin when a Christian sacrifices all else for church work? Fred is at every service and prayer meeting, on five committees, leads an evangelism programme, sings in the choir, runs the youth club, and edits the church magazine. Unsure if people will turn up for something? Fred will be there. Need a job done? Fred's your man. Desperate for encouragement? Fred'll give it. Fred is loyalty, faithfulness and commitment personified. His minister wishes he had more like Fred.

Fred's wife wishes she had a husband. She's on medication for depression, partly caused by loneliness. Fred's children used to wish they had a father, but by now they don't care. His son is taking drugs and his daughter clears out of the house to meet friends. Often neither of them bothers coming home for days.

Sometimes Fred mentions his family worries at the prayer meeting when they ask for topics to pray about. It occurs to no one that Fred's attendance at the meeting is partly the cause of the problem. If he'd given his wife and children the attention they deserved many things would have been different. They needed love – shared lives, not just words – but it was stolen away and given to everyone and everything else. God gave Fred a unique and great responsibility for just three people, and he sacrificed them. Does his church discipline him for that? Discipline? Fred's their hero. He gets sympathy, even admiration, for soldiering on in such a Christlike way despite lack of support from his family.

The sins of what we don't do

Perhaps the greatest number of unrecognised sins are of omission rather than commission. When an old woman lies ill with no one to care for her, who blames the Christian down the street for failing to notice that she's not out and about any more? When the man at the next desk gets unfair treatment from the head of department, who blames the Christian for busying himself with his work and not getting involved? When a neighbour's goods are sold to pay his debts, who blames the Christian for not helping financially? When a friend turns to eastern religions, who blames the Christian who for years was too embarrassed to tell him the gospel? So the examples could be multiplied. In truth, no one ever got thrown out of a church for what he never thought to do.

For most Christians, then, sin is cheating and lying, robbery and violence, lust and immorality. It's failing to believe, failing to pray, failing to keep the Ten Commandments. But sin is *not* things like driving too fast, making your home 'comfortable', getting locked into your favourite TV saga, chasing a career, building your business, giving excessive time to the church, or keeping too much of a distance from others. Most of those are never thought of as sins. Even when they are, they're not real sins.

An unbiblical distinction

The Bible lacks a distinction between real and unreal sins, those which must never be done and those which are acceptable either because they're not defined as sins, or because repenting of them would be too inconvenient. God is unimpressed by our self-suiting definitions and sense of convenience, and is more than a little bothered about things to which we turn a blind eye. Ten Israelite spies suffer a plague and die because they're negative about their people's ability to overcome the powerful tribes of

Canaan. Moses is barred from entering the Promised Land for a one-time failure to honour God in front of the people. Uzzah dies for steadying the ark of the covenant when it slips from its cart. Jesus ranks getting angry with a brother alongside murder, and says that calling someone a fool risks the fire of hell. Ananias and Sapphira are struck dead for exaggerating the size of their offering. None of those things were acceptable sins.

Neither does the Bible give any hint that the kinds of things we see daily from many Christians are acceptable. My church members who park illegally or friends who drive too fast would do well to ponder the early verses of Romans 13. 'Everyone must submit himself to the governing authorities, for there is no authority except that which God has established. The authorities that exist have been established by God. Consequently, he who rebels against the authority is rebelling against what God has instituted, and those who do so will bring judgment on themselves' (Rom. 13:1–2). Is breaking the rules of the road – yellow-line parking; doing 40 in a 30 m.p.h. zone – a real sin? Those Bible verses say explicitly that to flaunt earthly authority is to flaunt heavenly authority. God puts civil rulers in place to keep good order in society, so rebellion against their legitimate laws is rebellion against not just them but the one who appointed them. That's a real sin which really matters. It may be easy to escape or trivialise a parking or speeding fine. It won't be so easy to shrug off God's judgment.

Conformity

Those with lavish furnishings, state of the art electronic equipment, exotic holidays, and luxury cars are doing nothing worse than fitting into their society. What sin is there in that? A lot, actually. Christians aren't supposed to be like everyone else. We're not meant to blend in. 'Do not conform any longer to the pattern of this world . . .'

(Rom. 12:2). That includes worldly wealth as much as anything.

Of course, good evangelicals stress that, while they may have surrounded themselves with very nice things, they don't put their *trust* in them. Their trust is in God. Doesn't the Bible say that it's not money but the *love* of money which is a root of all kinds of evil (1 Tim. 6:10)? Yes, but the Bible is more realistic about human nature than most Christians. Only one verse before the warning about loving wealth, Timothy is told: 'People who want to get rich fall into temptation and a trap and into many foolish and harmful desires that plunge men into ruin and destruction.' There are no ifs or maybes there, for the blunt truth is that those who want wealth *will* fall into temptation. Once whetted, the appetite for 'nice things' is never satisfied. Ever increasing affluence becomes ever more important. In a hundred subtle ways, decisions are influenced by their wealth-generating potential. Wealth-diminishing options get rejected. The needs of others are secondary to self-interest.

In order that his disciples would avoid temptations like these, and well aware how people delude themselves, Jesus never talked about us *trusting* earthly treasures. He actually prohibited his followers from acquiring wealth. 'Do not store up for yourselves treasures on earth, where moth and rust destroy, and where thieves break in and steal. But store up for yourselves treasures in heaven, where moth and rust do not destroy, and where thieves do not break in and steal. For where your treasure is, there your heart will be also' (Matt. 6:19–21). Well-off Christians may argue that it's okay to surround themselves with comfort providing they don't love it or look to it for security, but Jesus was far harder and far more realistic. He said people's hearts *would* follow their treasure. If they had earthly wealth they would love it and would put their trust in it. They wouldn't be able to resist its pull. So he put an explicit prohibition on accumulating earthly resources. Rather, he said, invest in heaven.

It was precisely because of the reality that those with wealth will inevitably trust it, that Jesus told the rich young ruler to sell his possessions first and then follow him if he wanted eternal life. The man refused. Jesus did not lower the standard. He didn't say, 'What I mean is, you must be *willing* to sell all you have.' The man chose to keep his money, so Jesus let him walk away, unsaved. And he commented to his disciples, 'I tell you the truth, it is hard for a rich man to enter the kingdom of heaven. Again I tell you, it is easier for a camel to go through the eye of a needle than for a rich man to enter the kingdom of God' (Matt. 19:23–4). Is it acceptable for Christians to be materialistic? According to Jesus the price of wealth will almost certainly be the price of salvation.

Sabotaging our minds

Watching trash and trivia on TV may not seem much of a crime. Of itself it isn't. No one is sent to hell for having square eyes from hours in front of the set. But people are sent to hell for having lives controlled by sin. If in any sense we are what we think, we ought to be careful what we think. Only naïve Christians imagine themselves unaffected by what they watch. Even tiny streams eventually erode Grand Canyons. The erosion of the Christian mind ultimately destroys faith. Long before that it makes people less able to love rightly, think rightly, and act rightly.

We fight a spiritual war, and some lost battles are inevitable. At times temptation beats us, the enemy outsmarts us, persecution wears us down. In this fallen world, we don't always win. We have to come to terms with that. What is inexcusable, though, is entering the battle ill-prepared. If we're transformed by the renewing of our minds, without that renewal we'll inevitably conform to the world. Choices or actions which give us undisciplined minds become acts of surrender, defeat without fighting.

Paul urged Christians to be battle-ready: 'Finally, brothers, whatever is true, whatever is noble, whatever is right, whatever is pure, whatever is lovely, whatever is admirable – if anything is excellent or praiseworthy – think about such things' (Phil. 4:8). Christians are to fill their minds with good things. Anything less weakens us, a kind of self-wounding, as if the hardships of spiritual warfare weren't enough already. God wants his children fit. Sabotaging fitness matters to him. He calls it real sin.

Neglecting primary responsibilities

It's also a real sin when a career dictates its terms to everyone and everything around it. Who said it had to be like that? Perhaps God does lead some people to strike for the very top in business, and there's a considerable sacrifice of personal goals by those around them, especially by their families. But it's a dubious priority for *everyone*. Too many never question the assumed importance of getting the best qualifications possible, the best career possible, and reaching for the highest position possible in that career. Nor do they seem to notice the havoc they cause those near to them. When something takes controlling power in people's lives, something around which everything else has to be fitted, you call it their god. That's what a career has become for many, and they've followed that false god, supposing it was the right thing to do.

The Bible offers little comfort for those who neglect primary responsibilities, no matter the merit of the activities to which they divert their time and energy. Caring for families is primary enough that it's described as putting 'religion into practice' (1 Tim. 5:4). Neglecting family to do anything of personal choice amounts to abandoning the faith: 'If anyone does not provide for his relatives, and especially for his immediate family, he has denied the faith and is worse than an unbeliever' (1 Tim. 5:8). Although the context of that verse is financial, it is inconceivable that God would look on failure to supply love, attention, security, guidance, leadership (or any other family need) as being less serious.

That's why Fred is guilty if his wife and children have been made to suffer because he's neglected them. Being at church meetings and being busy with Christian activities were important responsibilities, but providing for the basic needs of his family were greater responsibilities. In God's eyes, to fail there was to fail significantly and foundationally. No parent is wholly to blame for how his children turn out. They grow up to make their own choices and are responsible for their own actions. Yet anyone who has contributed to their sin is held accountable by Jesus: 'If anyone causes one of these little ones who believe in me to sin, it would be better for him to have a large millstone hung around his neck and to be drowned in the depths of the sea' (Matt. 18:6). Those who think it a small thing to walk away from giving their children proper care should consider these words long and hard. Jesus thinks it a big thing, a very big thing.

Positive goodness needed

With other issues, too, the Bible is hard on Christians who don't act rightly.

Masters must treat their slaves fairly because they also have a Master in heaven (Col. 4:1). That probably means bosses who are unkind to their staff cannot expect kindness when they answer to the one who has power over them. As they have dealt with their employees, so they will be dealt with by God. Sobering thought for employers.

Those who fail to positively care for their neighbours or others might ponder the fate of the man entrusted with one talent of money. He buried the talent to make sure he could offer it back one day to his master. In other words, he never lost it, but neither did he use it. And for what he *didn't* do he forfeited everything (Matt. 25:14–30).

The same sin – failure by doing nothing – is there in what we call the parable of the good Samaritan (Luke 10:25–37). A traveller is assaulted and lies dying by the roadside. A priest and then a Levite both see him, but pass by on the other side. They fail the man. How? Did they attack him? No. Did they make his wounds worse? No. Did they ridicule him for being so stupid as to travel alone on a dangerous road? No. They fail him simply by doing nothing. Finally he is rescued by a Samaritan. And Jesus teaches from the parable that only the Samaritan was a neighbour to the man who had been wounded, for only the Samaritan did something to help him.

All too easily we miss the downside of this parable. In the end, did the inactivity of the priest and the Levite matter? The answer to that is a frightening yes, for they failed in something God required. The parable was told because a legal expert asked Jesus how he could have eternal life. What did the law say? It said he should love God and love his neighbour. But, the lawyer wanted clarification, who was this neighbour he had to love? The parable answered that by the model of the Samaritan's practical care for a hated but needy Jew. The Samaritan was the only one who did anything for the traveller. Both the priest and Levite passed him by. So, if eternal life required loving God and, in tangible ways, loving anyone else in need, the priest and Levite failed in half of what the law required. The simple deduction, then, is that they did not have eternal life. Their sin of omission mattered very much indeed, not just that one sin of course, but a way of life which showed them to be strangers to the love of God. What we don't do can be as significant as what we do.

Evaluating sin

Why do we think some sins aren't real sins? Many reasons, including the inconvenience and unattractiveness of giving them up. As well as that, we've drifted to evaluating sins by our estimation of the seriousness of their consequences. Some things have minimal or unseen consequences. So, parking on double yellow lines or pushing up the speedometer hurts no one. TV is merely entertaining fiction, since we're not *doing* the things we watch. Making our lifestyles comfortable is almost a virtue. Nothing seriously negative arises from these or many more things.

Yet there is harm, of course. Perhaps it's as simple as eventual parking anarchy, or as tragic as a death caused by a speeding car. Perhaps it's the gradual deterioration of our thought patterns, the sin born on some future day first conceived in our minds. Perhaps our materialism steals the resources which someone, far away and unseen by us, could have used to feed his family. We wanted them for comfort; he needed them for life. We don't take time, or don't care, to think through the consequences.

In any case, God doesn't evaluate sins by how great or small their consequences. Sexual immorality isn't wrong only when it results in an unwanted pregnancy; violence isn't wrong only when it leads to permanent injury; theft isn't acceptable when the money is taken from someone who's got plenty left. These things are wrong, always wrong, in God's eyes. Every sin is disobedience. Every sin is, to put it forcefully, rebellion against God's standard. It almost doesn't matter how much of a 'crime' something is or isn't on earth. Envy, jealousy or personal ambition don't seem great misdemeanours to us, but Paul lists them equally with immorality, debauchery, idolatry and witchcraft among the 'acts of the sinful nature' (Gal. 5:19–21). Likewise Jesus rated lust to be as bad as actual adultery (Matt. 5:27–8), and while we don't think anger much of a sin, as we saw earlier Jesus put it alongside murder and said that 'anyone who says, "You fool!" will be in danger of the fire of hell' (Matt. 5:21–2). 'Everyone who sins breaks the law; in fact, sin is lawlessness,' wrote John (1 John 3:4). Some actions aren't serious wrongs on our scale of values, but it's *God's* law which is broken. That's serious, always serious.

We've become complacent about the standards we accept. We've reckoned lots of things don't really matter or they're issues purely of personal choice. So, we chuckle about the church member with the reputation of driving so fast he's going quicker than his guardian angels. And we admire the person who sacrifices home and family life for his church commitment. Are these things acceptable? They're not. Along with many things like them they're sins – real sins – and all sins matter. No sins are acceptable.

Well, almost none.

I was leaving our church building one Sunday evening. Just up the street, on the double yellow lines, was a car belonging to one of the couples in our church. 'Right,' I said to Alison, my wife, 'I'll fix them.' I found paper and pen, and wrote a note, 'What about Romans 13:1–2?' I reckoned the Scripture passage might do them good, and I'd wrap the note round their windscreen wiper just like a traffic warden does with a parking ticket. As they walked towards their car, they'd think they'd been booked, and that thought might do them even more good. I scribbled out the message, and lifted the wiper to tuck the note underneath. I had not realised that the couple's Rottweiler dog was lying quietly on guard inside the car. The second I touched the wiper, enormous evil fangs lunged forward halting only a windscreen width from my fingers. I nearly went to heaven at that moment. Alison doubled up with laughter, and I was tempted to send her to heaven as well. The Romans 13 message never got left for that couple.

So I modify my conclusion. No sins are acceptable, but it's not wise to correct those who think their sins are, and have a Rottweiler to support their argument.

5

Long and late prayers work better

Tom and I were serious about knowing and serving God. We were fellow students at college, both Christians and both planning to enter the ministry. We needed a deeper experience of God, especially as we faced life-changing issues. 'Pray it all through' was the received advice. We knew what that meant: an all-night prayer meeting. That was the way Christians got answers at critical times. It was what Jesus did.

We began about midnight. We'd have started earlier, but all night is longer if you begin at nine o'clock and we weren't *that* keen. So midnight was fine.

For a while prayers flowed. We managed some praise, read some encouraging Scriptures, listened quietly in the silences, and then began to send a barrage of fervent requests in heaven's direction. This felt good. On and on we went. As all the greatest Christians seemed to say, time flew. Unaware of the minutes and hours streaking past, we were engrossed in laying hold on God. Our hearts were being poured out. One night would never be enough to fit in all we had to plead with God. Prayer followed prayer . . .

Finally my spiritual passion dipped enough to tempt a glance at my watch. Dawn must be about to break. Dawn was *not* about to break. It was hardly 12.30! Instead of six hours feeling like thirty minutes, thirty minutes had felt like six hours.

Nothing improved from that moment on. The prayers became shorter and fewer. The silences lengthened. My knees ached; my arms ached; my eyes ached. I remember thinking that I would be more comfortable if I reclined on the carpet. I remember nothing more until I felt Tom shaking my shoulder and saying, 'It's all right, Alistair, I've pronounced the benediction!' It was only 2 a.m., and I crawled off to bed knowing I was doomed to failure as a prayer warrior.

But was I? Why is praying for a long time better than praying for a short time? Must God be put under pressure before he'll agree? Are we to be like a petulant daughter whose technique to get her own way with her father is to browbeat him into submission? 'Okay,' he says finally, 'I give in. You can have what you want!' And why is praying all night better than praying all day? Do we imagine we'll catch God off guard if we pray out of normal working hours? Are we trying to slip our request into the heavenly answering machine at a time when God doesn't expect anyone to be calling?

Impressing God

Hopefully we're not driven by any of these quasi-theological and more than semi-heretical ideas, though our real motives may still not be too respectable. My suspicion is that we think God will prove more persuadable if we prove our love and dedication to him by sacrificing for him. Most people are impressed by sacrifice. It wins admiration and agreement. Why does a young man spend more than he earns to buy his young lady an expensive ring? He wants to show how much he loves her, and the gift is the proof. She'll see his sacrifice, her affections will be inspired, and she'll accept his proposal of marriage. Why shouldn't God be impressed in the same way? Our long or late-night prayers – our sacrifice of time and sleep – show God how committed we are to him and his will, hence he'll take us seriously and give us the answer we want. The logic is simple.

Of course, good evangelicals wouldn't admit to thinking like that. Their concern is to be biblical, and surely the practice of praying long and late is well grounded in Scripture? Some passages suggest it is.

Biblical basis

Particularly relevant to long praying is the parable of the persistent widow. Jesus told the story of a widow who was the victim of a wrongful ruling by an unjust judge. Faced with an unfair verdict, she wouldn't give up and pestered the judge for a better judgment. Still he wouldn't grant it. But she kept on, until he could stand her nagging no more and said, 'Even though I don't fear God or care about men, yet because this widow keeps bothering me, I will see that she gets justice, so that she won't eventually wear me out with her coming!' (Luke 18:4–5). The parable teaches clearly that Christians must not give up on prayer even when the answer doesn't come.

A second key passage specifies all-night prayer. 'One of those days Jesus went out to a mountainside to pray, and spent the night praying to God' (Luke 6:12). Jesus was faced with an important strategy decision. He prayed through the night and in the morning chose his twelve apostles. There are other references to late-night prayer. One follows the feeding of the five thousand. It had been a busy but triumphant day. When it was over Jesus sent his disciples ahead across the lake while he went into the hills to pray, and he stayed there well into the night. Jesus's prayers in Gethsemane mark another crucial occasion. His concentration on prayer late that night was intense, which is more than can be said for his inner core of apostles who kept falling asleep, an unfortunate precedent for prayer times.

So the emphasis on long and late prayer has Scriptural foundation. Or does it just *seem* to?

Constant prayer is what matters

Let's deal first with long prayers. There are biblical examples of prayers of reasonable length, such as Jesus's famous 'high priestly' prayer in John 17. However, what can't be found is any teaching to support the idea that a long prayer is more likely to get answered than a short one, that increased length leads to increased effectiveness.

The persistent widow parable has nothing to do with long prayers, as Luke's introduction to it clarifies: 'Then Jesus told his disciples a parable to show them that they should always pray and not give up' (Luke 18:1). The parable concerns *perseverance* in prayer. God doesn't want his people to give up when they don't see instant results. They're to keep their requests coming, not to toss one-off prayer requests in his direction which are then forgotten. Often a prayer must be put before God many times before it's answered. Jesus isn't saying we should persist with a single prayer until we get the answer. He isn't advocating putting all our prayer energy into one immense effort.

We could devise a parable of our own to illustrate that point. A temptation for today's affluent but hard-pressed parents is to buy their children lavish presents at Christmas to compensate for their lack of time and attention through the rest of the year. But, of course, one-off generosity is no substitute for everything which has been missed on a day-to-day basis. A healthy parent–child bond requires constant input. With that it grows; without it there is only decay and the eventual death of the relationship. Likewise, God has no wish for his people to give him lengthy but isolated attention once in a while, and then nothing. That diminishes the relationship, and devalues the topic prayed about. Instead, when an issue matters, God wants us to keep coming to him in prayer. Our commitment to the subject and to him are then clear. Jesus's promise is that when that happens, 'he will see that they get justice, and quickly' (Luke 18:8). So, *constant* prayer is the theme of the parable, not *lengthy* prayer. 'Pray continually' was Paul's way of saying the same thing (1 Thess. 5:17).

Misplaced trust

If a prime factor in prayer is the relationship behind it, there is another reason why protracted single efforts in prayer are precisely what God does *not* want. It ties in with a statement of Jesus specifically against lengthy prayer. 'And when you pray, do not keep on babbling like pagans, for they think they will be heard because of their many words. Do not be like them, for your Father knows what you need before you ask him' (Matt. 6:7–8). Jesus could not be clearer that long prayers carry no special powers. Many words are not more spiritually effective than a few. In fact – and here's the significant point – the implication in Jesus's statement is that many words *hinder* prayer because the seeker's trust is in the size of his prayer and not in God. He thinks he'll be successful because his prayer is so massive.

But God is not overpowered by verbosity, and failure to believe he'll hear and answer any sincere request reveals an impoverished relationship with God which must rob prayer of potency. Who can say how many elongated prayer times have been counter-productive because their very length put the emphasis on man's efforts at praying rather than God's love and power? Instead, God looks for confidence in him. Jesus taught people to hide themselves away secretly, and seek God and God's will sincerely. He would then give his perfect answer in his perfect timing (Matt. 6:6).

No preference for night-time prayer

What of late-night prayer? The Bible certainly has occasional examples of prayer through a night, or part of a night. They have one thing in common, though, and that's a context of crisis. In every case they occur at a time of urgency, pressure or emergency. So David fasted and presumably prayed through several nights while his newborn child was seriously ill (2 Sam. 12:15–23); Jesus sought the Father all or much of the night before choosing the apostles (Luke 6:12–16), during a chronically busy period of ministry (Mark 6:31, 46), and before going to the cross (Luke 22:39–46). And at least some of the early Church interceded into the early hours while Peter lay in prison and faced imminent execution (Acts 12:12). What do not appear in the biblical record are examples of people choosing night-time prayer on any grounds that the hours of darkness are more effective. Where people were deeply troubled, they called to God day and night. But no one opted to call to God by night in preference to day.

Any suggestion that the night-time hours are somehow better for prayer has one thing against it and one thing for it. Against it is a parallel danger to the one which occurs with long prayers, that someone may begin to trust the form or timing of the prayer for its power. There is no special spiritual efficacy about night-time. The air isn't thinner and God isn't less busy with other clients. Nor will God be persuaded of our commitment to pray simply because we do it late at night. We could be sacrificing comfort and sleep, but just as easily it could be evidence that we've no discipline with time-keeping. So anyone who thinks that night-time praying carries power in itself is guilty of putting trust in the wrong place. That's not the way to get prayers answered. A false reliance on late-night prayer is as counter-productive as a false reliance on lengthy prayer.

However, in favour of night-time praying is the potential for concentration on God because of the absence of other distractions. Life is unhelpfully hectic for many in today's chaotic world. There are people to see, letters to be answered, children to be cared for, deadlines to be met, journeys to be taken, friends to be visited, meetings to be attended. The inner spirit gets stressed, and focusing on God becomes ever harder. The mind keeps barging in with reminders of the next job which must be done. There's always something or someone clamouring for attention. In practice it's near to impossible for many to find time or privacy for the secret prayer encouraged by Jesus (Matt. 6:6). But, at 2 a.m. phones don't ring (usually), the boss doesn't shout for the project which is overdue, nor does Aunt Ethel expect us to call. The night offers solitude, and that precious commodity of uninterrupted time. Our hearts can be quiet, and our spirits tuned heavenward. When else could we give God such undivided attention? When else would we listen to his still small voice whispering deep in our souls? We need quality time with God, and late at night may be the only readily available option for that. And when a crisis strikes, and God's will or power must be found, night-time prayer may become the essential spiritual lifeline.

So the tranquillity of the late hours brings opportunity to concentrate on God. That alone is the benefit of prayer at night, for there is no hidden power about nocturnal prayer. Nor is there a spiritual turbo boost by praying at excessive length about something. It's a myth that long and late prayers are more effective.

I faced one of the biggest decisions of my life. Friendship had blossomed into romance, and that romance had brought me to the brink of commitment. But was Alison *the* one? I needed the answer, and felt I needed it now. Late that night I finished my cocoa, got down on my knees, and closed my eyes. This was going to be serious intercession. I would pray through the night, and keep praying until God spoke. Words were few as I stumbled out my pleadings with God. Yet, I consoled myself, my words weren't important, for the real purpose was to be quiet and listen for what God had to say to me. I must have listened a little too passively. My eyes stayed closed for hours. I woke to find it was 3.30 a.m., and I was still on my knees. With an excruciatingly painful protest from my limbs, I stretched. Should I keep praying? Maybe I should, but I couldn't. The spirit was still willing, but the flesh was all too weak. Bed and proper sleep were irresistible attractions. Once more I had failed as a prayer warrior.

Well, maybe not, for I slept soundly for the rest of that night, woke with a clear head, and knew exactly what I had to do. And being married to Alison has been one of life's greatest blessings down the years since. There are moments when God's answer is to stop long or late praying, and get on and do what is plain and obvious.

6

Even the bad times are good

Sarah was a good mother, and the friend she met in the street distracted her attention away from her four-year-old son, Andrew, for just one minute. But it took only that minute for Andrew to allow his ball to roll on to the road, and for him to run after it. A deafening squeal of brakes wrenched Sarah's attention back. As her head spun round, she heard a sickening thud, and she saw her small boy's life end under the wheels of a bus.

The panic and grief of that moment hardly dimmed in the days and weeks that followed. Inevitably, Sarah blamed herself for what had happened. 'If only I'd held his hand . . . If only I hadn't stopped to talk . . . If only I hadn't allowed him to have his ball . . . If only the bus hadn't been passing at that moment . . .' But no amount of 'If onlys' changed anything. Nothing now would bring Andrew back. Sarah was devastated.

Sarah was a Christian, and had wonderful support from her many friends. They cried with her, prayed with her, phoned to encourage her, and did thoughtful things like baking a cake to brighten her life a little. Their care was appreciated. But that wasn't the case with everything they *said*. And they said plenty. Some statements were helpful; some were not. Nearly all of them offered one particular piece of counsel, 'Sarah, you must realise that although this accident seems so bad, it'll be all right eventually. God has good reasons why this has happened. He'll make Andrew's death a blessing in your life.' When she shook her head slowly in disbelief, they quoted their Scriptural basis: 'We know that all things work together for good to them that love God' (Rom. 8:28). Fight off doubt, they told her. It might take time, but some day she would find God's purpose in all this.

Sarah was not comforted and did doubt. Far from helping, her well-meaning friends increased her agony. How could it have been good for Andrew to have his life ended so early and terribly? What kind of God would think it was good for Sarah to have her son die? She could not and would not believe that the accident was meant. If God considered this was what she really needed, then he was a perverse tyrant, and she would not put her trust in such a God. Even if, somehow – and she could not see it – there was some hidden end which was good, how could there be justification for achieving it by such terrible means? Her son's death, and the counsel of her friends, threw Sarah into a spiritual wilderness.

Seeking a purpose in hardship

When there is any tragedy or hardship, the simple truth that trips off the tongues of many Christians is that God makes even the bad times good. It was told to me over and over again when I was hospitalised twice in six months because of a slipped disc in my back. It could hardly have come at a worse time for I had just moved home to begin a new ministry. I preached one sermon to the congregation, and that was all for eight weeks while I lay flat in agony. I recovered from that difficult time, only to be off for another twelve weeks later. Plenty of people phoned, wrote, or visited to let me know they cared, that they were praying for me, and that God had everything under control. They said he really must want to teach me something to lay me aside like this, for, after all, he works everything together for good. I lay in my hospital bed and wracked my brain wondering what I could have missed which was so important that God had to do this to get my attention. I stared at the ceiling, and wished God would take a giant paintbrush and write on the roof whatever message or lesson my dim brain was failing to grasp. If only God would let me see it so that the suffering could come to an end. As weeks became months, I felt about as successful as the prophets of Baal on Mount Carmel: 'There was no response, no-one answered, no-one paid attention' (1 Kings 18:29).

Sometimes I risked suggesting to a visitor that perhaps there *wasn't* some great purpose behind my pain and disability. A suspicious eyebrow would be raised, and I would be told, very lovingly, 'Don't resist God, Alistair. I'm sure that once you really put your life in his hands, you'll find what he's trying to teach you, and then you can find your healing.' In other words, learn or suffer. To question whether God had a purpose in my illness was evidence that I was missing or rejecting the purpose, and my ordeal would go on.

When I did eventually get well, people rejoiced that God's plans had obviously been fulfilled. I protested I hadn't had any great revelations nor could I see anything good about losing nearly half a year's work, but they reckoned that even though I couldn't list them, deep inside I must have learned new truths and I would be the stronger for that. I hope I was, because those months away allowed some serious problems to develop in the church which made my eventual start in the new ministry much more difficult. If that was good, the benefit was lost on me.

Joseph's experience

Those who champion 'even the bad times are good' theology have a hero in the Old Testament in the person of Joseph. The story is familiar. His brothers were jealous, had Joseph kidnapped, sold into slavery and taken to Egypt. His father thought him dead, and his brothers hoped never to see him again. Joseph was bought by Potiphar, worked hard and became head servant for the house. But just when his fortunes seemed to be recovering, he became the target for the sexual ambitions of Potiphar's wife. He refused her advances, and she vented her spite by falsely accusing him of sexual assault, and Joseph was thrown into jail. He did well there, though, and soon was running the prison on behalf of the warder. During that time he interpreted dreams, including one which helped Pharaoh's cupbearer. In gratitude the cupbearer should have put in a good word for Joseph when he was released. But he didn't; Joseph was forgotten. For more than two years Joseph languished in a stinking dungeon.

Then Pharaoh had dreams which no one could interpret. The cupbearer finally remembered Joseph. The prisoner was sent for, successfully told Pharaoh the meaning of his dreams, and his counsel to place a wise and discerning man over Egypt was fulfilled by his own appointment. Joseph was plucked from prison and placed in the palace; from one of the least in the land he became one of the greatest, second only to Pharaoh himself.

The Bible does not record all this merely to tell a story of skulduggery with a happy ending. It's what happens next that matters. Back in Canaan Joseph's family were starving, but news came that there was grain in Egypt and the brothers went to buy. They didn't recognise Joseph in his royal robes, and at first he hid his identity from them, and put them to the test. This time they refused to sacrifice a brother. Joseph must have felt they had learned a lesson, and revealed who he was. They were overwhelmed, and more than a little afraid. The brother they had all but murdered was now in a position to do whatever he pleased with them. This time *their* lives were in *his* hands.

But Joseph refused to blame them for what they'd done, for, at a deeper level than they knew, God was behind their actions.

And now, do not be distressed and do not be angry with yourselves for selling me here, because it was to save lives that God sent me ahead of you. For two years now there has been famine in the land, and for the next five years there will not be ploughing and reaping. But God sent me ahead of you to preserve for you a remnant on earth and to save your lives by a great deliverance. So then, it was not you who sent me here, but God. (Gen. 45:5–8)

Joseph had never wanted to be attacked, deported, become a slave, or get thrown into jail. He would have wished simply to stay Jacob's favourite son back in Canaan. Once a slave, he would have preferred to stay head of Potiphar's household. But – he saw now – God's plan could not be fulfilled with him in either Canaan or Potiphar's home. The various moves in his life were intended to get him into the royal palace in Egypt, make him ruler there, and thus save his family from starvation. If ever all things worked together for good, it was in the life of Joseph.

With backing like that, it's not surprising the words of William Cowper's old hymn have achieved near canonical status:

> *God moves in a mysterious way,*
> *His wonders to perform;*
> *He plants His footsteps in the sea,*
> *And rides upon the storm.*
>
> *Judge not the Lord by feeble sense,*
> *But trust Him for His grace;*
> *Behind a frowning providence*
> *He hides a smiling face.*
>
> *His purposes will ripen fast,*
> *Unfolding every hour;*
> *The bud may have a bitter taste,*
> *But sweet will be the flower.*

Black Friday is Good Friday

If final proof is needed that even the bad times are good, then evangelicals look no further than the story of Jesus himself, and in particular to his crucifixion. In mankind's history it was the greatest act of criminality and wickedness and yet also the greatest act of justice and virtue. What should be called Black Friday is Good Friday, as Christ's suffering and death achieved man's redemption.

What happened to Jesus seemed wholly evil. It looked as though Satan had won the day. Yet Christ's death was the will of God, for through it the consequences of Adam's sin were undone: '. . . just as the result of one trespass was condemnation for all men, so also the result of one act of righteousness was justification that brings life for all men' (Rom. 5:18). From one perspective his death was negative and the devil's work, but from another it was positive and the act of God. 'God was reconciling the world to himself in Christ, not counting men's sins against them . . . God made him who had no sin to be sin for us, so that in him we might become the righteousness of God' (2 Cor. 5:19, 21).

Jesus's death was bad, but really it was good. The hate against him, the false accusations, the beatings, the crown of thorns, and the nails through his hands and feet, were all terrible. But there was a purpose, and through Jesus's sufferings we are forgiven. It was worth it because of what it led to.

So likewise for us. We face some terrible things. Perhaps in time they'll make sense, or maybe they'll never make sense this side of heaven. But we can trust God. He will always have a reason for what happens. No matter how bad some times are, really they're good.

A comforting theology?

There is considerable comfort in all this for many. Humbly granting themselves no more than what Cowper called 'feeble sense', they don't feel they have to understand everything. All they must do is trust. A train driver approaching a busy station isn't responsible for working out which of the maze of tracks is his, but can have faith that a skilled signalman, with an overall view and plan, will switch the points to put him on the right line. In the same way we must believe God knows what he is doing, and no matter how hard the path on which we find ourselves it must be right.

Others, like Sarah with whom we began, are less comforted by this theology if it means she has to accept her son's death was a good thing. If, using the analogy of a train approaching a station, the points were switched to direct the incoming train down a line which took it straight into another train already at a platform, and dozens of innocent passengers were killed, who would blame the driver (if he survived the crash) for questioning the competence of the signalman who sent him down the wrong line?

Are bad times really good times? What is the truth and what is the myth?

Many errors are nearly but not quite right. They're not a lie, but not exactly the truth either. So with this one.

God at work to do good

To start with the truth, it is unnecessary and wrong to question Joseph's conclusion that God was at work through his captivity and deportation to Egypt, and used a variety of circumstances to bring him eventually to virtual rulership over the land and thus to save his own family. Joseph hadn't understood it while it was happening, but still it happened. None of his brothers, nor Potiphar's wife, nor the cupbearer, nor Pharaoh had any consciousness of co-operating with God, yet every one of them was. God was active, anticipating and planning for their every action. Only later did Joseph see that God had been in it all. Eventually he told his brothers, 'You intended to harm me, but God intended it for good to accomplish what is now being done, the saving of many lives' (Gen. 50:20). He was quite right in that conclusion. God had been moving in a mysterious way, his wonders to perform.

In fact two things are clearly true. First, actions and events that seem and are truly bad can lead to good results. Thus a barbaric, unjust and illegal crucifixion becomes the means of salvation for all, even for those who plotted Jesus's death or drove the nails into him. Second, no matter how dark and evil an event, and how terrible its effects, God is there and at work to do good through it. There is no part of life from which he is absent. There is no time when he is inactive or acts for anything other than the well-being of his people. '"For I know the plans I have for you," declares the LORD, "plans to prosper you and not to harm you, plans to give you hope and a future"' (Jer. 29:11). Always that is true.

However, two other things are also true.

First, God does not do evil. No matter how good the *end* could be, God never stoops to using *means* which are bad. His actions are always pure and right. Second, simply because there are instances where dreadful circumstances or experiences have led to good outcomes, it does not follow that there must be a hidden purpose of good in every tragedy. Bad things may be no more than that: bad things.

God does not do evil

The first of these truths should be self-evident and basic in any Christian's theology. Holiness, purity and goodness are foundational attributes of God. The seraphs in heaven called, 'Holy, holy, holy is the LORD Almighty' (Isa. 6:3), leaving Isaiah feeling unclean in God's presence. 'True and just are his judgments,' proclaimed another heavenly chorus (Rev. 19:2).

The fact that God is utterly flawless and therefore can never act improperly was not lost on his biblical servants

on earth who several times pointed it out to him in their
prayers. Most notable of these was Abraham. He was
forewarned about the imminent destruction of Sodom,
and became concerned in case there were good people in
the city as well as bad, and all were wiped out together.
That could not be right. So Abraham told God:

> Will you sweep away the righteous with the wicked?
> What if there are fifty righteous people in the city?
> Will you really sweep it away and not spare the place
> for the sake of the fifty righteous people in it? Far be
> it from you to do such a thing – to kill the righteous
> with the wicked, treating the righteous and the wicked
> alike. Far be it from you! Will not the Judge of all the
> earth do right? (Gen. 18:23–5)

It was inconceivable to Abraham that God could do
wrong by giving a universal judgment when some were
innocent. The just nature of God made that impossible.
Abraham was right, and God agreed with him.

A good God cannot act badly. Joseph saw God's hand
at work in what happened to him, but that does not mean
God inspired his brothers to sell him, or Potiphar's wife to
want him for sex. God does not will assault and kidnap.
God does not inspire lust and immorality. He cannot act
against his own nature of holiness, no matter how good the
outcome would be. Therefore God does not send toddlers
to their deaths under the wheels of buses, nor push lumbar
discs out of place, just to teach people a lesson. To say he
does is near to blasphemy, making God the author of sin
and evil.

God uses what's evil

What God does do is make use of sin and evil to serve his
own ends. When my children were small I wanted them to
learn how risky it was to go near a fire. How was I to do

that? Of course I told them the dangers, but I knew children aren't the best of listeners and a pre-emptive lecture would not be enough. So, the obvious thing to do was to take a child's arm and thrust it into the flame. The pain and shrivelled skin would teach him a lesson he couldn't forget. He'd never go near a fire again. But, of course, I didn't do that. I could never inflict such an injury on anyone, and certainly not a child I loved. Yet the day came when one of my children reached out carelessly towards flames. Before I could react there was a burn, thankfully tiny and trivial. And that became the moment when my words were really learned by my child, as I drummed the lesson home to him alongside the comfort of hugs and ointment. I didn't want him hurt. He hurt himself. But I used his pain to teach him about fire so he'd be spared any greater hurt of that kind.

In countless ways like that God uses the evil of this world to serve his purposes. Sometimes, like I did with my son, it's to teach a lesson. Sometimes it's to bring people to a place of repentance and a fresh start. Sometimes it's to demonstrate his power through rescue and change. Sometimes, as with Christ's death on the cross, he transforms the effect of evil and makes it work for his own ends. God does not cause evil, but he does use it.

God's work is always good

God at work to bring good into the midst of evil is, in fact, nearer the correct understanding of Romans 8:28. Perhaps out of wishful thinking, it's the Authorised (King James) Version of that verse which is always remembered with its promise that 'all things work together for good to them that love God'. Who would not want that to be true? We almost need to believe there must be a hidden good or purpose in the bad things of life. It may be the only positive thought which keeps us going when disaster strikes.

But C.H. Dodd calls the old rendering 'a serious mistranslation' and 'not an admissible rendering of the

Greek' (*The Epistle of Paul to the Romans*, The Moffat New Testament Commentary [Hodder & Stoughton, 1932], p.13). Few modern translations reproduce its line of thought. The Revised Standard Version says: '. . . in everything God works for good with those who love him'. The Good News Bible has almost identical wording to that. The New English Bible and Revised English Bible say: '. . . in everything, as we know, he co-operates for good with those who love God'. The New International Version has: '. . . in all things God works for the good of those who love him'. The Contemporary English Version phrases it: 'We know that God is always at work for the good of everyone who loves him.'* These translations do not make the verse say that all things either are good or will become good. The promise is rather that *God's* work in our lives and tragedies is always good and for our good, no matter how bad other factors might be.

When my young daughter fell on to rocks, I thought at first she was dead. After fifteen agonising seconds of silence, she cried. It was wonderful! But she was hurt and distressed. I comforted her, carried her to safety, and then laid her in the car and drove as fast as I dared to the nearest hospital. On the way she vomited, and I had to stop to help and reassure her. Eventually she passed out, and I had to cradle her in my arms as I hurried into the emergency room. After some days in hospital she recovered. It took me far longer! Through every stage of that trauma, I – her father – worked for her good. I cared for her in her pain, encouraged her she would be all right, and got help for her. That didn't make the accident good. The fall on to rocks was bad, entirely bad. But into the badness I brought all the good a father could make possible.

---

* Exceptions among newer translations are the New Revised Standard with an AV-sounding 'all things work together for good for those who love God', and the New Jerusalem Bible's promise to Christians that God 'turns everything to their good'.

That's what Paul is teaching God does, and of cou ˙ almighty and all-loving God can bring a degree of goodnes greater than any human father can give his child. Bad things happen in a fallen world. God does not will them, but into the midst of evil he comes with his grace and strength, bringing goodness to the lives of his children. Sometimes that goodness is comfort, sometimes healing, or strength to keep going, or forgiveness, or hope, or any other of his blessings. In all things, no matter how terrible, God is at work for the good of those who love him.

That understanding removes God from being the author of evil. It also allows us to abandon the view that there must be a hidden purpose of good in everything. Evil can happen simply because evil happens. In this fallen world not everything works the way its Maker intended. If an old-fashioned clock – the kind with wheels and cogs – got dirt in its works then the whole thing went wrong, not just the part that was directly contaminated. Because every component was interconnected, even 'innocent' parts ran slow or stopped working. It wasn't the fault of the good components. But it happened. And the evil in this world can mean suffering and hardship even for innocent people. It's not the fault of the innocent that they suffer nor is it the will of God. If we must blame anyone we could try laying responsibility on Adam and Eve for their first sin, though perhaps only the perfect of this world should ever judge others, and none of us qualify.

Bad times are always bad times

The world is not out of God's control, though he has allowed us to spoil it. One day he will call all to account, but not yet, for he wants many more to find forgiveness. Until the final day of reckoning comes, we will live in a broken and damaged world, one in which we may experience harm and hurts never intended by our loving Father.

The way to come to terms with that is not to attribute

to God. Nor is it to believe against
must be something good about evil,
lly. And we ought not to be so cruel
for someone's ongoing suffering on
sp the lesson God must be wanting to

A ponse to tragedy is to see that God is with
us while e going through it, consistently giving grace
and strength. We are not abandoned, and God will bring
whatever good is possible out of our pain and hardships.
Sometimes the balance between good and bad in an event
will be on the side of bad, for ultimate justice and restoration
are not experienced by us this side of eternity. Yet, at other
times, we will find a surprise round the corner, and discover
that God used what was so terrible to bring something much
better to pass in our lives.

Even the bad times are good? No, they're not. Bad times
are always bad times, and it's wrong to pretend otherwise
and unfair to offload responsibility for them on to God.
Thankfully the truth is that no matter how bad the bad
times get, God never gives up on us. He keeps on patiently
and persistently working for one goal, 'the good of those
who love him'.

7

Real Christians begin
each day with a quiet time

Long flowing robes, Bible grasped in one hand while the
other punched the air dramatically, a voice that carried
for miles, and crowds in tears of repentance. That was
my hero, George Whitefield, and his ministry shook the
nation. Surely God wanted to use me to shake the nation
too. So my hero would be my model. The gestures could
be learned, the voice could be trained, and presumably the
robes were optional. So what was missing? To my horror I
read somewhere that my hero George rose at five o'clock
every morning to pray for three hours. I was all for prayer,
but not pre-dawn. Why couldn't his secret have been that
he got extra strength for ministry by having a lie-in each
day? But if early-morning prayer was what it took to be
God's man to reach a nation, I'd do it.

The alarm hand of the clock felt stiff as it was forced
towards the number 5, protesting at such an unnatural time
setting. As I crawled into bed at midnight I wondered how
I'd survive on only five hours' sleep. 'God will increase
your strength,' came an inner voice. It had to be divine
reassurance.

Anticipation of the alarm meant sleep was light. I dozed
and wakened, dozed and wakened. The luminous clock
hands crept past 2. My eyelids fell shut, but opened again
to see 2.45, and then 3 and a little later 4. Finally I found
deep sleep. The 5 a.m. crescendo in my ear could have been

a bugle from hell. But as I thumped the alarm into silence, I convinced myself it was summoning me heavenward and rolled out of bed. It was still dark outside. Just to be up at that time of day must mean I was getting more spiritual.

I prayed, I sang songs, I read the Scriptures. When I'd exhausted that, I read the Scriptures, sang songs, and prayed. Six o'clock dragged past. I snatched a cup of coffee to keep me going. George Whitefield wouldn't have needed it, but sanctification is a gradual process and this was only day one. By the time seven o'clock was reached I reckoned I'd prayed for everyone I'd ever known. Even my dead dog had had a mention. I covered a few of my more notable prayer requests a second time. It felt like underlining their importance to God. There were still thirty minutes to go. With nothing left on my agenda, I fetched my hymn book and read out the hymns to God. It seemed a good mixture of praise, intercession and even confession. Reading them was a lot better than singing by that stage, and with 800 hymns in the book I wasn't likely to run out. Again I looked at the clock. It was five past eight! I'd made it. I had prayed for three hours. New degrees of holiness oozed from every pore. I ate my breakfast with pious joy, and went into the day confident of God's presence and power like I'd never known before. When plans worked out, I knew they were God's answers to my prayers. When they didn't, I knew they were trials that God would now give me grace to bear.

I was tired that night. Very tired. Actually I'd been tired right through the day, and hadn't finished all I had to do. So, with body maintenance prolonged by caffeine infusions, I sat up late finishing my work. But nothing would persuade me not to set the alarm for five o'clock again. Deep sleep enfolded me within ten seconds of getting horizontal. It seemed one minute later that the 5 a.m. siren sounded in the distance. My hand stretched out and quenched its screeching. Eyes closed again. Something stirred me an hour later. I leapt out of bed feeling guilty and disappointed for oversleeping. Two hours of prayer just wouldn't be enough to become a spiritual giant. I didn't manage even two hours. The mistake was to kneel by my bed. At 8.15 searing pain in my knees woke me from an hour and a half extra sleep in my crouched position. Breakfast was not eaten with pious joy. God seemed very distant that day. When plans worked out I was grateful that I hadn't spoiled everything. When they didn't, I knew it was because I hadn't prayed as I should.

I was too exhausted to work properly that day, so I had to stay up late again that night to get finished. The prospect of another early rise excited me as much as the thought of a bath in cold porridge. But I had to try. Once more I set the alarm for five. I never even heard it. The loudest bugle either hell or heaven had in stock could have sounded, and it wouldn't have roused me. George Whitefield would remain unique. I staggered into that day around eight, managed a few minutes of hasty prayer, including a desperate plea for God not to abandon me just because I hadn't prayed adequately.

God never had any intention of abandoning me. His presence or absence that day would have nothing to do with how much or how little prayer had been offered in a quiet time. In fact it would not even have anything to do with whether or not I had had a quiet time.

The daily quiet time

Standard evangelical wisdom, however, places a high value on the daily quiet time. There can hardly have been an evangelistic booklet which, after getting the person through the prayer of commitment, does not go on to emphasise the need for the new Christian to set aside a specific period for prayer each day. Usually early morning is advised, before the hustle and bustle of the day crowds it out. It's a chance to bring the plans of the day before the Lord, and pray the details through. Nearly always the example of Jesus is quoted. 'Very early in the morning, while it was still dark, Jesus got up, left the house and went off to a solitary place,

where he prayed' (Mark 1:35). What better model could
there be? If Jesus began each day with prayer, it's obvious
that we should too.

Morning prayer was not originated by Jesus. The writers
of the Psalms were early risers. 'In the morning, O LORD,
you hear my voice; in the morning I lay my requests before
you and wait in expectation' (Ps. 5:3). 'But I cry to you
for help, O LORD; in the morning my prayer comes before
you' (Ps. 88:13). Time with God is put before anything and
everything else by these people.

Thus the Christian learns that an early-morning quiet
time with God is biblical. It also seems right. Prayer is
given its proper priority, and God is honoured because
we talk to him while our minds are fresh. After a quiet
time, the day can be entered confident of God's blessing
and power.

All of that sounds so sensible, so Scriptural and so
spiritual. But is it any of those? Those whose brains don't
get out of neutral before 11 a.m. might question how sensible
or honouring it is to present their befuddled minds to God at
dawn. That's not the only question which should be asked.
Did Jesus really begin every day with our kind of quiet
time? Is prayer the priority to which God calls us? Far from
making a Christian more spiritual, could a daily quiet time
actually push someone further away from God?

Superstition and ritual

Sadly, the reality is that quiet-time theology has degener-
ated to the level of crass superstition or ritualism, often
controlled by powerful feelings of guilt or fear. There's a
prayer time to be got through in the morning. Do it and the
day's a winner. Don't do it and the day is doomed before
it's begun.

Joe thinks like that. It's Monday morning. His Bible
study guide tells him the four verses he must read that day,
so he does. He moves on to prayer. Joe is really organised,

and has a prayer list. He recites the day's people, problems and projects to God, asking for a blessing on each. Fifteen minutes later he finishes. Into the day he goes, glad to have got his priorities right. If you met Joe later and questioned him about what he had learned from his Bible reading, he'd look blank and might not even remember what the passage was. If you asked what changes he expected his prayers would make, he might be surprised. Changes? If you wondered what he'd heard God tell him, he'd smile quizzically. What a strange thought . . . But, as far as Joe is concerned, everything's fine. It's a good day. He had his prayer time.

The tragic heresy of Joe and many like him is that their trust is in their prayer time, and not in God. Because Joe said his prayers, he believes all is right with God. Even put kindly, that's dangerous, unbiblical nonsense! The act of prayer has almost no value in itself. Many times in the Bible God condemns empty ritual. Detached from a right relationship with him, offerings, sacrifices and even prayer are worthless. He told the people of Malachi's day, 'Oh, that one of you would shut the temple doors, so that you would not light useless fires on my altar! I am not pleased with you . . .' (Mal. 1:10). God's word through Isaiah is no less severe. 'When you spread out your hands in prayer, I will hide my eyes from you; even if you offer many prayers, I will not listen' (Isa. 1:15). The Bible's teaching is that there is no merit in a quiet time, not if it is an end in itself. Often that's all it is.

Did Jesus have a quiet time?

What matters is not the quiet time but meaningful contact and a right relationship with God. Prayer certainly helps achieve that. Hence Jesus taught the importance of private prayer (Matt. 6:6), and sometimes went away from others in order to get time on his own to talk to his Father. Immediately after the feeding of the five thousand, Jesus

sent away both the crowd and his own disciples, and when
he was alone he prayed (Mark 6:46). At another time he's
described as 'praying in private' even though his disciples
were nearby (Luke 9:18). Probably the best-known example
of Jesus at prayer is in Gethsemane. Facing the imminent
agony of the cross, 'He withdrew about a stone's throw
beyond them, knelt down and prayed' (Luke 22:41).

So, Jesus was a man of prayer, and private prayer at that.
But did he have a morning quiet time? The answer is yes
and no.

It's 'yes' because the best historical evidence tells us most
Jews said prayers twice a day, and one of those times was in
the morning. The other was either in the afternoon or in the
evening. Some prayed while still lying in their beds. Some
prayed while having a morning wash in the sea. Others
prayed wherever was most suitable for them. There's no
reason to think Jesus did not include traditional Jewish
ways into his fuller life of prayer, and that means he prayed
in the mornings.

But he didn't have a quiet time as we know it, for there's
no evidence that he made one big prayer investment per
day. Ask good evangelicals how often the Bible describes
Jesus getting up early to pray, and most will say, 'Many
times'. They're wrong. The correct answer is just once.
The instance quoted before from Mark's gospel is the
only occasion Jesus is ever mentioned as praying early in
the morning. In fact, when Luke is describing the same
incident, he doesn't even mention prayer. 'At daybreak
Jesus went out to a solitary place. The people were looking
for him and when they came to where he was, they tried
to keep him from leaving them' (Luke 4:42). For all the
detail Luke supplies, Jesus could have been admiring the
view, enjoying the sunrise, or having his breakfast in peace.
What makes Luke's omission of prayer significant is that,
of all the gospel writers, he's considered to be the one
who puts special emphasis on prayer. Did he not know
Jesus prayed that morning? Maybe he didn't, in which

case it wasn't a much talked-about detail. Or he did, in which case it wasn't so important that he thought it worth mentioning. Neither explanation suggests that a morning prayer time was a feature of overwhelming prominence in the routine of Jesus's day.

The gospels actually record Jesus as doing several different things early in the day. For example, Jesus is the original commuter. 'Early in the morning . . . he was on his way back to the city' (Matt. 21:18). So, he travelled first thing. He also got to work early: '. . . all the people came early in the morning to hear him at the temple' (Luke 21:38). 'At dawn he appeared again in the temple courts, where all the people gathered round him, and he sat down to teach them' (John 8:2). If Jesus did many things, why do evangelicals pick prayer out of the list of his dawn habits as the obligatory practice to copy? Why not something else? If the gospels had mentioned Jesus stretching his limbs as he woke from a night's sleep on hard ground, we could now be telling everyone that early-morning aerobics is biblical.

As far as we've been told by the gospel writers, it seems Jesus prayed more frequently at night, such as on the mountainside or in Gethsemane, or just prior to choosing his apostles. 'One of those days Jesus went out to a mountainside to pray, and spent the night praying to God. When morning came, he called his disciples to him and chose twelve . . .' (Luke 6:12–13).

All day prayer

References to early-morning prayer by the Psalmists are descriptive rather than prescriptive, and should not be overrated. Partly they're just further examples of Jewish customs. Partly they reflect a need during crisis circumstances. Of course David prayed in the morning. He was facing great troubles. They pressed deeply into his mind, and as he thought about them he prayed about them. But that wasn't only in the morning. David prayed at all points

of the day: 'O my God, I cry out by day, but you do not
answer, by night, and am not silent' (Ps. 22:2). Some of his
most fervent praying was through the hours of darkness
while lying on his bed: 'I am worn out from groaning;
all night long I flood my bed with weeping and drench
my couch with tears . . . Away from me, all you who do
evil, for the LORD has heard my weeping. The LORD has
heard my cry for mercy; the LORD accepts my prayer' (Ps.
6:6, 8–9).

Psalm 88, quoted earlier, mentions morning prayer but
only as part of the greater truth that prayer is to be offered
at all times. Its opening verses contain testimony to all-day
prayer: 'O LORD, the God who saves me, day and night I
cry out before you. May my prayer come before you; turn
your ear to my cry' (Ps. 88:1–2).

'Pray continually'

The Bible simply doesn't teach the principle of a once-a-day
quiet time. What it teaches is many-times-a-day quiet times.
Prayer will happen for us first thing in the morning, again on
the way to work, perhaps during a morning break and then
around lunch-time. So the process will continue through the
rest of the day, ending probably with prayers being offered
while lying in bed waiting for sleep. In a sense prayer will
never have stopped from waking to sleeping. Undoubtedly
there will need to be some form of discipline to reserve
certain parts of the day to give God our full attention.
The rest, though, is equally lived in his presence, a kind
of day-long conversation with God, running through every
activity.

That pattern fits with what the Bible commands
about prayer. Paul put it succinctly in his letter to
the Thessalonians: 'pray continually' (1 Thess. 5:17). The
advice of the letter to the Ephesians is a little more wordy,
but has the same stress on constant prayer: 'And pray in
the Spirit on all occasions with all kinds of prayers and

requests. With this in mind, be alert and always keep on praying for all the saints' (Eph. 6:18).

The Bible nowhere teaches people to invest everything in one daily audience with God nor to value one part of the day for prayer more than others. It teaches unending prayer, moment-by-moment openness, part listening and part talking.

Dangerous deception

The greatest danger of the quiet time is how easily it can take people away from God. The very thing which ought to bring them to God may keep them from him.

Like Joe. He had his quiet time every day, and felt better for it. He shouldn't have. Only real contact with God should have satisfied, and he'd had little or no real interaction with God. But the quiet time had been enough. The ritual had substituted for God as the source of his spiritual strength for that day, a sadly insufficient source. And poor Joe doesn't even realise he's allowed the quiet time to replace God. He'll find out only if he wonders why, despite all his praying, he still feels so far from God. At the moment, he's got something in common with steam-train enthusiasts. They seek out old rolling-stock still running on private tracks, book their ticket and go for a journey, enjoying the smoke, the smell and the jolting ride. Ask them, 'Where did you go on the train?' and they won't care. They may not even know. Being on the train was all that mattered; they didn't need to go anywhere. For these enthusiasts, the original goal of the train, to take people to a destination, has been superseded by contentment merely to be on the train. That's what's happened with quiet times. For the 'Joes' of the Christian world, quiet times don't have to take the person anywhere. They don't have to reach God. The quiet time itself is all that matters.

What a dangerous deception that is. We're fooled. We think our prayer times are making us more holy, bringing

us more spiritual power, and pleasing God. They aren't.
We're being fulfilled by the means and not the end. Satan
must love it. By making us satisfied by prayer we never
reach God himself. Thus we settle for a poor substitute for
the reality God wants.

The real priority

What does God want? Despite what countless preachers say,
prayer is not the priority that God seeks. What God wants
from and for his people is fellowship, a shared relationship,
a loving closeness.

Even in the old covenant that was understood. Belonging
to God and having fellowship with him was at the core of
that covenant. God told the Israelites, 'I will walk among
you and be your God, and you will be my people' (Lev.
26:12). The Song of Songs described that relationship in
the language of two lovers, so intimately in places that no
preacher dares read out those passages in church. The Bible
can be too hot for sacred ears! Here are two safe extracts:
'My lover is mine and I am his' (2:16); 'You have stolen
my heart, my sister, my bride; you have stolen my heart
with one glance of your eyes . . .' (4:9). The couple feel
deeply and passionately for each other. Their song expresses
the relationship between Israel (or the Church) and God.
God wants fellowship, a love affair, with his people. The
prophets also found tender words to convey God's intimacy
and affection: 'The LORD your God is with you, he is mighty
to save. He will take great delight in you, he will quiet you
with his love, he will rejoice over you with singing' (Zeph.
3:17). The imagery could be of a gentle mother crooning
her little child to sleep with love songs. Closeness with his
people, a shared existence, is what God wants.

This intimacy is no less in the new covenant. The early
Christians understood they were a 'chosen people . . . a
people belonging to God' (1 Pet. 2:9). That's not mainly a
'legal' belonging but one of close fellowship: 'We proclaim

to you what we have seen and heard, so that you also may have fellowship with us. And our fellowship is with the Father and with his Son, Jesus Christ' (1 John 1:3). Fellowship with him was God's purpose in salvation. 'God, who has called you into fellowship with his Son Jesus Christ our Lord, is faithful' (1 Cor. 1:9). At the risk of overstating it, we can say the God of love needs people to love and needs a freely given love in return. Love cannot accept a forced response. So, as people enter willingly into faith, they enter into a relationship of mutual love with God. That relationship is what God wanted when he first made the world. Restoring it is fundamental to what salvation is about.

Therefore it's not prayer which is God's priority for us, but intimacy, fellowship, oneness, a loving relationship. Prayer is a means to that end, but not the end itself. When a quiet time becomes the god, and our trust is placed in having satisfied that god, we fail to have fellowship with the true God.

Every moment openness

How can our loving relationship with God grow? What will make it vibrant and fulfilling? Certainly not a once-a-day blitz conversation, especially since it isn't usually a conversation but a one-sided monologue. If all the attention my wife got from me was ten to twenty minutes' worth first thing in the morning, our marriage would be in trouble. Based on my semi-comatose input at 7 a.m., I wouldn't fancy its chances. Thankfully, there's much more to the relationship than that. We often talk on the phone at some point during the day, share news over the evening meal, perhaps do something together in the evening, and have a longer and deeper conversation last thing at night when the children have finally disappeared to bed. Our ideal is constant communication.

There are times, of course, when communication is far

from constant. Sometimes work is highly pressurised. I'm out every evening, get home exhausted and not much in a mood for conversation. Sometimes I travel, and I can be out of touch with Alison for several days. That doesn't end my marriage, because the marriage depends on the relationship, not on our communication. Of course we restore communication as soon as possible – it feeds the relationship – but our marriage is not in tatters simply because we have had little contact for a few days. Yet good Christians are riddled with guilt if one prayer time with God is missed. And they're afraid God won't be with them if they haven't had their quiet time. This mechanistic concept of prayer – put your prayer in the early-morning slot if you want God's blessing to pop out the drawer at the bottom – treats God as a machine, instead of the loving Father who longs to share the whole day with his children.

What God wants is not quiet times. He wants his children living in a relationship of love with him. That cannot be built on one period of prayer per day, whatever time it's at. It can't even be built on prayer. It's something for every moment of time, and involves not only words but also attitudes and actions as everything about us flows from our relationship with him and becomes an offering to God. There's a constant openness, constant devotion, constant dependency, constant sharing of every thought, need and experience.

Does this make prayer unimportant? Not at all. Prayer matters, because it's a principal means of relating to our heavenly Father. Take away the means and you don't reach the end. To use the earlier analogy, you don't get to the destination if you don't get on the train. I don't object to the train. I object only when people think it's enough merely to be on the train for a little while each day, forgetting where that train is supposed to take them.

There's no biblical basis for putting prayer into a once-a-day slot. And the evangelical exaltation of quiet times has bred a misplaced trust in them, as if God's nearness and power for a particular day rested on the presence or absence of prayer in that day. Our relationship with God is much greater than that.

My praying now doesn't happen in a single burst. I use the main sections (morning, afternoon, evening) and major events (appointments, meetings, tasks) as triggers for special prayer. Thus every day has a rhythm of prayer which fits naturally with my lifestyle. As well as that I'm praying informally in the midst of noise and hassle throughout the day. There's a sudden crisis, and I'm shooting a prayer heavenward. Something good happens, and I'm breathing my thanks to God. A problem isn't getting resolved, and I'm talking it through quietly with my Father. I'm reading the paper and praying for the news reported there. Prayer can be almost endless.

I don't get up for prayer at 5 a.m. any more. Would I be holier if I did? Not a chance. I'd be utterly exhausted, thoroughly irritable and not even remotely Christlike. Nowadays, of one thing you can be sure – 5 a.m. is a very quiet time for me, very quiet indeed.

8

You become a Christian by asking Christ into your life

Mary was confused. At just six years of age, she'd heard that Jesus loved her and wanted to be her friend. That was nice. She had lots of friends at school, but Jesus was going to be her special friend, her biggest friend, her most important friend. She wouldn't be able to see him, but he'd always be with her. She could talk to him anytime, and he'd help her. She hoped he was good at sums.

Everything was fine, except her Sunday School teacher was telling her she had to ask Jesus to come into her heart. 'If you say a little prayer asking him to come and live right inside your heart, he'll do it.' The teacher smiled; Mary frowned.

Mary looked across at a painting of Jesus – tall, blond, white robe, moving confidently but gently among little children. She loved that picture, and wanted this Jesus as her friend. But . . .?

'What's wrong, Mary?' her teacher asked, seeing the hesitation and frown.

'He's too big.'

'Too big? What do you mean?'

'Jesus is too big to get into my heart.'

Thankfully the teacher didn't laugh, but patiently tried to explain that Jesus today doesn't have a body like we have, but it's his Spirit who would come and live in Mary's heart. Now Mary was confused even more, for she didn't know what a 'spirit' was. But like any six year old, she trusted her teacher so she asked Jesus to come into her heart. It was good to have him as her special friend.

Perhaps it doesn't matter that a child gets confused when she's told to ask Jesus to come into her heart. As far as we know (though who has bothered to find out?) the jargon doesn't ultimately put many off.

Praying to ask Jesus into your heart, or into your life, is the standard evangelical formula to become a Christian. Crusade counsellors are trained to lead an enquirer through a prayer of commitment. Evangelistic booklets contain a sample prayer that the prospective convert can use. Preachers often finish a gospel message with an invitation to 'pray after me to invite Jesus into your life'. Becoming a Christian is a matter of praying for Christ to come in.

Christ in us

The Bible certainly teaches that a Christian is someone in whom Christ lives. 'I have been crucified with Christ and I no longer live, but Christ lives in me,' Paul writes (Gal. 2:20). Converse statements that describe the believer as being 'in Christ' are far more common – 164 times in some form of words (in Christ, in him, in the Lord) in Paul's letters – but the two glorious truths are there: we are in Christ and Christ is in us. A fish is in the sea and (as it breathes water through its gills) the sea is in the fish. The ocean or river is the fish's whole environment. So it is for the Christian with Christ.

Jesus also gave his disciples similar teaching before he left them.

And I will ask the Father, and he will give you another Counsellor to be with you for ever – the Spirit of truth. The world cannot accept him, because it neither sees him nor knows him. But you know him, for he lives with you and will be in you. I will not leave you as orphans; I will come to you . . . Because I live, you also will live. On that

day you will realise that I am in my Father, and you are
in me, and I am in you. (John 14:16–20)

Jesus mingled statements about the Spirit with statements
about himself, with the result that there seems no significant
difference between speaking about Jesus or the Spirit being
in the Christian.

Other passages have much the same theme:

You, however, are controlled not by the sinful nature
but by the Spirit, if the Spirit of God lives in you. And
if anyone does not have the Spirit of Christ, he does not
belong to Christ. But if Christ is in you, your body is
dead because of sin, yet your spirit is alive because of
righteousness. And if the Spirit of him who raised Jesus
from the dead is living in you, he who raised Christ from
the dead will also give life to your mortal bodies through
his Spirit, who lives in you. (Rom. 8:9–11)

For we were all baptised by one Spirit into one body –
whether Jews or Greeks, slave or free – and we were all
given the one Spirit to drink. (1 Cor. 12:13)

. . . the one who is in you is greater than the one who is
in the world. (1 John 4:4)

So, providing we allow for mentions of the Spirit, the New
Testament has no lack of references to the indwelling Christ.

'Come into my heart, Lord Jesus'

If the New Testament gives a biblical basis for evangelicals
to talk of Christ living in them, probably their songs have
popularised the doctrine. A whole generation has been
raised on lyrics in which Christ being in us is a strong theme.

> *Into my heart, into my heart,*
> *Come into my heart Lord Jesus,*

Come in today, come in to stay,
Come into my heart, Lord Jesus.

It's no longer I that liveth,
but Christ that liveth in me . . .
In me! In me!
Jesus is alive in me!
It's no longer I that liveth,
but Christ that liveth in me.

He lives, He lives,
Christ Jesus lives today.
He walks with me,
He talks with me,
Along life's narrow way.
He lives, He lives,
Salvation to impart.
You ask me how I know he lives?
He lives within my heart.

Songs are a powerful teaching medium. Sung over and over, truths are imbibed which become the background framework of thought. In this case there's nothing wrong with the conclusion reached. From Scripture and songs, evangelicals rightly hold strongly to the belief that Christ lives in them.

So where's the problem? There are two when the Christ in me doctrine becomes part of a standard evangelistic methodology for becoming a Christian.

An unbiblical invitation

First, there is no biblical basis for telling an upcoming convert to ask Christ into his life. More than that. Not a single person in the New Testament ever says a prayer in order to become a Christian. Not in the gospels, Acts or the letters does it happen.

The Day of Pentecost converts 'accepted his message'

(Acts 2:41), the first Samaritan Christians were said to have 'believed' and to have 'accepted the word of God' (Acts 8:12, 14), and Cornelius and household to have 'received the word of God' (Acts 11:1). Similar phrases are used elsewhere for other conversions. Sometimes actions, such as baptism or Zacchaeus giving away half his goods to the poor, are visible signs of change. There's a variety of New Testament responses, but the one that never appears is anyone hearing the Christian message and giving his life to Christ by means of a prayer.

The nearest we get to prayer at conversion is from Paul. Ananias urges him, 'And now what are you waiting for? Get up, be baptised and wash your sins away, calling on his name' (Acts 22:16). To order Paul to call on Christ's name seems like an instruction to pray, but probably isn't. More likely, he's being told to use or trust in the name of Jesus for the forgiveness of his sins as he undergoes baptism. (That's similar to Peter's command to the crowd, 'Repent and be baptised, every one of you, in the name of Jesus Christ for the forgiveness of your sins' [Acts 2:38].) Paul certainly didn't think Ananias was asking him merely to bow his head and invite Jesus into his life.

Does it matter that no one in the Bible ever prays to become a Christian but we've made it the standard method? Mostly it doesn't, providing we never insist that 'pray to ask Jesus into your life' is a formula that someone must follow in order to be saved. The New Testament pattern is that there is no pattern for the 'mechanics' of being converted. There is no right or wrong method. We mustn't think, 'Maybe Joe's not really a Christian. He never prayed a proper prayer of commitment.' Joe didn't need to pray, nor does anyone else. It may be helpful for people to voice the commitment they're making, but it's not the speaking out of that commitment, by prayer or any other form of words, that makes a conversion secure. What matters is 'believing', 'accepting the word of God', and so beginning a new life in a right relationship with Christ.

Dave was converted right in the middle of a school class. The teacher was talking about religion, and asked if anyone took the Christian faith seriously. For some reason, in front of everyone, he asked Dave directly, 'Tell me, Dave, do you believe in Jesus?' Dave had been going to church all his life, but he'd never made a personal commitment. Now, in school, he was being asked if he really believed. Later he described his response like this: 'Right at that moment, with the teacher waiting for a reply, I decided I did believe in Jesus, and I did trust him with my life. So I said firmly, "Yes, I believe in him." From then on I was a Christian.' And he was. There was no prayer, but the commitment made in that class was for life.

Since the New Testament does not require prayer for conversion, no one else has the right to insist on it. Praying for Jesus to come into your life is not *the* way but *a* way to become a Christian.

On the brink of an abyss?

There is a second and more serious problem with the 'ask Jesus to come into your life' formula. It may be theologically accurate to speak of Christ being in our lives, but that doesn't mean it's appropriate for someone becoming a Christian to ask Christ into his life. 'Asking' is too polite, too tame!

Take these scenarios.

- My doorbell rings. It's one of my neighbours, returning the lawnmower I loaned him the other day. We chat for a moment and then I ask, 'Would you like to come in, perhaps have some coffee?' I'm being kind, neighbourly, friendly. I don't have to invite him in. I can merely take back my lawnmower. But my neighbour is a likeable chap, and I enjoy his company, so I ask him to stay for coffee.

- I'm climbing a mountain. It's spring but there's still snow at the altitude I've reached. Traversing a treacherous slope, I'm roped to my friend for safety. I pause to catch my breath and adjust my climbing harness. Thinking my footing to be secure, just for a moment I unhitch my rope. It's a near fatal mistake. My boot slips and in an instant I'm sliding and tumbling down the hill. Just thirty metres below me is a cliff edge. If I go over it, nothing will break my fall for 1000 metres. In desperation I dig in my ice axe. It slips. It won't grip. The cliff edge is only metres away. I roll over and throw all my weight on that axe. Still it cuts through the snow until, suddenly, with a jerk that nearly pulls my arm from its socket, the axe pick bites and I'm stopped. Nervous, frightened to move because I'm unsure how firmly that axe is driven into the icy snow, I glance below. I am one metre from the edge, hanging on the lip of a precipice, my feet already dangling in space. Somehow – and quickly – I have to get back to safety. But the slope down which I've fallen is a forty degree wall of ice that I'll never climb. I seem doomed to die. Even as that terrible thought registers, the ice axe slips an inch. I force it down again, but I know my weight will soon be too much. Whether next second or next minute, it'll break free. There's just one chance – my friend! 'The rope!' I shout to him. 'Throw the rope!' Being pulled to safety is my only hope. 'Throw the rope, throw it now . . .'

In the first of these little cameos, I decide I would enjoy my neighbour's company, so I invite him into my home. In the second, I'm nearly plunging to my destruction, and scream for my friend to save me. Both involve asking something from another person. Yet there's a totally different mood, urgency and importance with the second asking compared to the first. It'll be nice if my neighbour accepts my invitation, but it doesn't really matter if he declines. But I *need* my friend on the mountain to throw the rope. I'm appealing to him because I'll die if he doesn't rescue me.

The non-Christian is in a plight not unlike mine on the mountain. He's on the brink of an eternal abyss, and catastrophe could come at any moment. Like my need of my friend, his need of Christ is everything. Jesus is his only hope. Nothing else matters. Knowing my danger I didn't call to my friend like I spoke to my neighbour. I almost begged him to save me quickly before it was too late. It is with that sense of need that people ought to come to Christ. They must have him; they cannot live without him.

Those who are invited merely to ask Jesus into their lives are given a false impression. That form of words understates the importance of what they have to do. Instead of reaching out to Christ with urgency, aware of their desperate need of a Saviour, they ask Christ in with the sense, 'My life would be better to have Jesus in it. I'd be enriched.'

Many things are brought into people's lives to enrich them. 'I've never been the same,' says Arthur, 'since Helen came into my life.' 'I'm fitter, stronger and more able to face this world since aerobic exercise came into my life,' says Diane. Or, since a new hobby, new sport or new car came into their lives, others are boosted in some way. Very easily Jesus is ranked alongside these things. He's the newest piece of furniture, to be enjoyed and valued since he improves the quality of life, but ultimately only one thing among many. Perhaps, because he is the Son of God, he's the best and most important addition to life, but still only a new accessory, something to want because he's good to have.

But Christ can never be merely 'good to have', one of the wants of someone's life. I have many wants, some of which are even needs: sunshine and fresh air, exercise and a healthy diet, company from friends and family, a reasonable pace to life, good employment, better time management, eight hours' sleep each night. But at the moment of hanging on to a cliff edge by only an ice axe, I have a need for my mountaineering friend and his rope which is qualitatively different from all those. My need of rescue is in a vastly higher league from everything else I think of as a want or need in my life. So it is with our need of Christ.

We must have him, not to make us feel better, but to rescue us. We've gone too far and can't save ourselves. Having Jesus in our lives is not an optional extra. He is now our only hope. If he doesn't stretch out his hand to us, we're lost. If we don't put our entire trust in him, we're doomed. So we don't politely ask him to come as an add-on to our lives, we cry, 'Come quickly, save me before it's too late.'

Christianity as a hobby

Have we bred a generation of church members for whom Christianity is little more than a hobby? Just as other things have come into their lives, so they have brought Jesus into their lives. Being a Christian is a major or minor pastime. Some organise much of their time round Christian activities, while others can be bothered only when they have a sense of need or the mood is right.

Christianity is only a hobby . . . Is that an exaggeration? Perhaps, yet too many who once prayed for Christ to come into their lives don't value him. They have little appreciation that without Jesus they're lost, little awareness that they must grasp daily his outstretched hand, little commitment to him as Saviour and Lord of their whole lives. Instead Jesus is fitted in where convenient, like asking the neighbour to stay for coffee if you enjoy his company.

We're sending wrong signals to people by telling them to give Jesus a polite invitation into their lives. It's too ordinary, too much like the way we take up other things. Accepting Jesus must be radically different.

Is this just semantics, just a matter of words? Not when those words determine what is believed. Our words to the prospective Christian are signposts. According to what we tell him he knows what is expected. If it's only 'Ask Jesus into your life', he may tragically fail to realise his real need and the real importance of Jesus. He makes Jesus part of his life, just as many things have become part of his life. It may be near Christianity but not near enough.

Christ comes to live in us as we come to live in him. As Christ totally surrendered his life for us, so we totally surrender our lives to him. That's biblical teaching. What is not biblical is anything less, and the standard of commitment pointed to by the counsel to 'Ask Christ into your life' is often sadly lacking.

9

The answer must come, for so many are praying

Karen died. She had been talented, vivacious and a wonderful example of Christlikeness. We all rejoiced with Karen and her husband when their second little girl was born. We shared their shock a couple of months later when Karen was diagnosed with cancer. They prayed as a family, I prayed with them, the whole church prayed for them. Karen was widely known and much loved, and the news of her condition spread quickly. Many others in churches over a wide area began to pray. Hundreds prayed for Karen. Concerned friends passed her name down telephone prayer chains. Before long it was being said, 'We know Karen will be healed, for there are so many people praying for her now all over the world.' Within six months Karen had wasted away and died, leaving her husband, two little girls less than two years of age, and many sad and puzzled people. Eventually thousands had prayed for Karen. Why hadn't God answered?

That question has been asked many other times after the Christian army has been mobilised to pray. The motivation for such widescale prayer could be a national crisis. Maybe an election is due. Perhaps new legislation is being considered which particularly concerns Christians. It's vital that God's people intercede. A call to prayer like that went out in England when there were proposals to allow shops to open for business on Sundays. Campaigns were mounted, and Christians everywhere stirred to pray against the new trading laws. Around the same time there were bills before Parliament concerning abortion and homosexuality, and they provoked another national prayer campaign. Christian leaders put out an appeal, 'We need as many as possible to pray!'

When David Watson became ill with cancer in 1983 many were moved to pray for his healing. This great Anglican preacher's ministry had touched countless lives and he'd taught so many about God's power. He was bound to be miraculously healed. The critical need was to get enough people to pray. All over the world Christians pleaded with God. He was well known and loved in Britain, the United States, Australia and other countries. News came that in Zimbabwe, a country he had never even visited, thousands were praying for him. It was typical of what was happening wherever Christians had heard of his condition. These prayers were not reluctant nor half-hearted, but sincere and infused with faith. Surely, with such a man and with so many calling on God's mercy, David Watson must be made well.

His death in 1984 came as a great shock. It didn't make sense. Nor did it make sense that Sunday trading laws were liberalised, the legal age for homosexual practices was lowered, and abortion was not significantly restricted. A huge number of good Christian people had prayed, but the answers they wanted hadn't come.

God ought to have done something. Why? Because David Watson's ministry should have lasted longer, the Lord's Day should have been preserved, homosexuality should be held in check, and abortion is an evil. The people who prayed would have given those reasons. But not just those. God ought to have answered their prayers because so many prayed. They agreed together in prayer, therefore God should have granted their requests.

'If two agree, it will be done by my Father'

Jesus's teaching is critical.

> I tell you the truth, whatever you bind on earth will be
> bound in heaven, and whatever you loose on earth will
> be loosed in heaven. Again, I tell you that if two of you
> on earth agree about anything you ask for, it will be done
> for you by my Father in heaven. For where two or three
> come together in my name, there am I with them. (Matt.
> 18:18–20)

Where people gather together in the name of Jesus, and
are in agreement about a matter, then God has pledged to
answer their prayer. If that's true when just two or three
bring their united request to God, surely it must be even
more true if two or three thousand, or perhaps two or three
hundred thousand, all present the same request to God?

Hence prayer chain ministries have mushroomed. A
prayer need is phoned to a local co-ordinator. That contact
passes the request to the next person down the line, and
so, call by call, along the chain it goes. Perhaps within
minutes there'll be a dozen concerned Christians praying
through the problem. If the topic is of special importance,
one of the chain will be linked to a wider, regional network
of prayer chains. If the item is of national concern, then
it will be passed to all the networks in the country. By
now thousands of people on hundreds of prayer chains
could be interceding. Finally, if the issue is of sufficient
magnitude, a national prayer co-ordinator will channel it
to international contacts, and it will be prayed for on chains
in many countries round the world. The final number of
people praying is vast. The boost to telephone companies'
profits is also huge. So why do it? The whole *raison d'être*
is that the more who pray the more likely the prayer is to
be answered.

The same logic exists with the desire for revival. Revival-seeking prayer meetings are set up across the country. Some are early-morning. Some are late-night. Some are city-wide. Some are in local churches. Some are short-lived. Some have gone on for years. People get together to call on God to send revival to their community or their land. Often they'll meet at the same time as similar groups in other localities. Perhaps whole days or nights are set aside for prayer. Or a twenty-four-hour period is divided into blocks of time, and people are urged to pick one when they promise they'll be at prayer. 'That way,' the organisers enthuse, 'we know every moment of the day has someone praying for revival.' Question why that's important, and you're asked, 'When has there ever been a revival without the cry of God's people going heavenward?'

Rescue followed prayer

Biblical backing is claimed by those who argue for wide-spread prayer. The first major 'revival' in history – the rescue of God's people from Egypt – began with nationwide prayer. 'The Israelites groaned in their slavery and cried out, and their cry for help because of their slavery went up to God. God heard their groaning and he remembered his covenant with Abraham, with Isaac and with Jacob. So God looked on the Israelites and was concerned about them' (Exod. 2:23–5). Then God called Moses, and sent him back to Egypt to set his people free. The nation prayed, and liberation came.

Something similar happened a few generations later when the Israelites, by then in their promised land, were suffering invasion after invasion from Midianites. The crops were ruined, their animals slaughtered and the people forced to hide in the mountains. They had disobeyed God, and they were suffering for it. But the suffering drove them back to God. 'Midian so impoverished the Israelites that they cried out to the LORD for help. When the Israelites cried to the

LORD because of Midian, he sent them a prophet . . .' (Judg. 6:6–8). Very soon God was not only sending a prophet but commissioning and inspiring Gideon to lead an army into battle against the Midianites. The nation prayed, and God saved them.

Thus Christians conclude that where there's a major need there must be a major effort in prayer. If a nation is drifting away from God, the nation's Christians had better cry out to God for it. If a church wants to see God at work it should get its members mobilised in prayer. When few pray little is expected to happen. When large numbers pray there's anticipation that God will act.

The logic is simple. The more who pray the better chance that God will answer that prayer.

Deciding God's will for him?

But what kind of rationale and theology lies behind all this? What kind of God is moved or unmoved according to the number we can motivate to pray? What kind of power are we presumed to have over God?

I saw a cartoon some years ago. A church committee is gathered to do business. A serious-looking chairman addresses them, 'If I understand our constitution rightly, it requires a two-thirds majority to overturn the will of God.' What many have come to believe about prayer is nearly that. If enough Christians can all present the same request before God then he's obliged to grant that request. It's as if we're saying, 'Where there's a two-thirds majority, then God's will is decided for him.' Of course no one would want to put it in those terms, but it's the unspoken logic behind the drive to get more and more people all praying about the same topic.

This myth creates enormous pressure. If someone's sick, it may not be enough that one or two pray in faith, or that merely the elders gather for prayer. As many others as possible must all pray. An evangelistic event won't succeed unless armies of prayer warriors are on their knees. Misguided legislation needs every Christian praying against it if there's to be any chance of it being changed. The dread is not getting the right result because not enough people have prayed. Yet, how many are 'enough'? No one can say, but the nagging fear is that it could be just a few more than the number we've got praying. That generates an insatiable desire to get ever more people praying. If something turns out badly, the guilt is enormous. Maybe it would have been different if only we'd got more to pray.

Two facts would seem to militate against the survival of this myth. One is the simple reality that many prayers are not answered, at least not in the way people want, no matter how many are praying. I remember a whole church uniting in fervent prayer when Mike, a prominent member, was diagnosed with terminal cancer. He was a much loved man, with a wife and children who loved him and needed him. Surely it couldn't be God's will to take Mike? Everyone prayed. Over and over they prayed, and so did many more Christians throughout the city and beyond. But even though so many prayed, they didn't get the healing they asked for. Mike died. Countless other issues have had undesirable conclusions even though they were also much prayed for. That happens often enough to make you think folk would give up the idea that healing (or any other answer) is bound to come if only enough pray. Strangely it survives.

Second, the longevity of the myth is surprising because it stands in direct contradiction to at least one other cherished view, the enormous power of just one person's prayers. Revival folklore treasures stories of great movements of the Spirit in a community which have come about because of the prayers of a single individual. 'Old Jenny prayed for her town for fifty years when no one else cared. The place was a den of iniquity. Hardly anyone bothered with church any more. But Jenny prayed for her neighbours, for the school teachers, for the young people, for the civic leaders. She never gave up. And God blessed her prayers by sending a revival. Now there are hundreds in church each week, some of the bars have closed down due to lack of business, and the courtroom is the quietest place in town since there's so little crime. All because one faithful old woman prayed . . .' That's how the stories go, and they're wonderful. If they're true, then they're a powerful antidote to the teaching which requires lots of people to be praying before God answers.

Why, then, do we go on thinking that if only lots of people will pray there's a greater likelihood of God saying 'yes'? The answer probably has two parts. To some extent it's a biblical misunderstanding. To a greater extent it's an unthinking anthropomorphising of God.

Misunderstanding

Biblically, the famous 'where two or three come together in my name' passage from Matthew 18:20 is critical, with its immediately preceding statement that what two on earth agree and ask for will be done for them by the Father in heaven (Matt. 18:19). Jesus seems to give validity to the idea that the effectiveness of prayer is increased when a higher number do the praying.

If Jesus had been referring to prayer, that might have been his meaning. But he wasn't. What Jesus was teaching his disciples was how to resolve disputes between Christians and, at this point, what to do when someone refuses to accept he's in the wrong: '. . . if he will not listen, take one or two others along, so that every matter may be established by the testimony of two or three witnesses' (v.16). That was the Jewish law. Deuteronomy 19:15 said no one could be convicted of a crime solely on the basis of one witness's statement. Evidence agreed on by two or three was needed. Jesus was laying down the same principle for church disputes. If, following the agreement of the two or three on the facts of the case, the individual still will not accept the judgment, Jesus says the church is to disassociate itself from him (v.17). But the consequences of that are more than merely loss of fellowship, for Jesus says the decision made on earth will be recognised in heaven (v.18). His heavenly Father will do what two on earth agree, for Jesus will have been with those two or three when they made their decision (vv.19–20).

That's strong teaching, and (unsurprisingly) theologians have more than one understanding of what Jesus meant. Yet almost all agree that the context of his words is church discipline. In some way Jesus was promising heavenly backing for an earthly verdict on an unrepentant church member. It would become more than merely an earthly verdict, for Jesus would be in their midst when they reached their judgment.

So, prayer (as simplistically defined) is not what Jesus was talking about in Matthew 18:20. Isolate these words from their context, and they can be taken to mean prayer is effective in proportion to the number praying. Put the words back into context and there's no such justification, for Jesus wasn't talking about praying to God for anything.

The other biblical passages mentioned earlier are really no better in giving support to the idea that 'the more who pray the more certain the answer'. Certainly Exodus 2 mentions people crying out because of their slavery. Interestingly neither that reference nor those in the following chapter actually says the Israelites were praying. They groaned and cried out for help. We're not told whether their cry was directed at God for divine rescue, directed at their slave masters in hope of mercy, or was merely the more general, untargeted, agonising lamenting of oppressed people. But God heard them. The writer of Exodus stresses God's pity for his people, and his recalling of the covenant promises. 'God heard their groaning and he remembered his covenant with Abraham, with Isaac and with Jacob' (Exod. 2:24). Thus God decided to intervene and Moses was found.

The LORD said, 'I have indeed seen the misery of my people in Egypt. I have heard them crying out because of their slave drivers, and I am concerned about their suffering. So I have come down to rescue them from the hand of the Egyptians and to bring them up out of that land into a good and spacious land, a land flowing with milk and honey – the home of the Canaanites, Hittites, Amorites, Perizzites, Hivites and Jebusites. And now the cry of the Israelites has reached me, and I have seen the way the Egyptians are oppressing them. So now, go. I am sending you to Pharaoh to bring my people the Israelites out of Egypt.' (Exod. 3:7–10)

The pronoun 'I' appears a remarkable number of times in those verses. Here is God making a sovereign intervention based on the compassion he feels and the promises he has made. God's decision to act on behalf of his people is what lies at the heart of the Exodus rescue. Yes, the Israelites cried out. But God's salvation of them is never portrayed as something brought about by the united turning to God of these people.

Nor did that really happen with the people of Gideon's day, even though this time the Israelites did cry out specifically to God. In response God sent a prophet among them first and rescued them later through Gideon. However, to summarise the story that way is misleading. These were not repentant people now desperately seeking God. And God didn't treat them as if they were. For example, the prophet made no promises of help to them. In fact, he told the people that they'd only themselves to blame for being in such a mess. God saved them from slavery in Egypt and gave them victory over enemies when they occupied their new land. God's word through the prophet continued: 'I said to you, "I am the LORD your God; do not worship the gods of the Amorites, in whose land you live." But you have not listened to me' (Judg. 6:10). That was his message, and nothing more. His job was explanation, not liberation, and he was clearly talking to unrepentant people who were well out of touch with God. And they hadn't improved one bit by the time rescue began with Gideon. He was almost put to death after he carried out his first task of demolishing an altar to the false god Baal and a pole in honour of the goddess Asherah. A lynch mob demanded that Gideon should be handed over to die for what he'd done, and only his father's pleading saved him. Here was Israel – God's people – irate to the point of wanting blood because someone had destroyed the symbols of their false gods. Not exactly a legitimate spiritual fervency! The fact that they were eventually saved from the Midianites was hardly God's response to their faithful praying.

These biblical passages don't teach that prayers become more effective when many people pray. In fact the Bible never makes an issue of how many ask God about anything. Asking according to God's will is relevant. How many do the asking is not.

Outvoting God?

Perhaps the real train of thought behind the 'so many are praying the answer must come' mentality has little to do with anything biblical, and almost everything to do with ideas of how to get things done in modern Western societies. Unthinkingly we may have constructed our theology from our systems of democracy.

Suppose I want the law changed. I might think it environmentally better to ban all motorised transport from the centre of my city. How am I going to achieve that? Nothing will change just because Alistair Brown wants it. Why should legislators pay attention to him? If there's to be any possibility of a change in the law, there'll have to be a massive groundswell of public opinion in favour. So I start my campaign. I contact the press, organise meetings, distribute leaflets. I talk about carbon monoxide poisoning from cars and buses. I emphasise the benefits to health of walking or cycling. I stress the number of accidents to pedestrians knocked down by cars and buses on crowded streets. Gradually people come round to my way of thinking. The local cycle club agrees that banning motorised traffic is a wonderful idea, leaving the roads clear for cyclists. Some shopkeepers are attracted by the thought of pedestrians sauntering up the street, stopping to buy as they go. Ecology groups see this as an essential step to stemming environmental pollution. Support builds. I make appointments with local civic leaders. They've heard of my campaign, and they take me seriously. They don't talk to me as someone representing merely his own views. They know many others think this way too. If they still won't change the law, I step up my offensive. I work out even more arguments to ban traffic. Buildings will look cleaner. Wildlife will return to city parks. We won't be deafened in the main streets. We can get rid of hideous traffic lights. Our shoes won't be contaminated by oil stains when we cross the road. I'm changing public opinion. The momentum builds. I circulate a petition. Hundreds put down their names. Then thousands. I'm winning the argument. Eventually well over half the population of my city sign up. I make another appointment with the local politicians, and pull a cart to their door with my petition of several hundred thousand signatures. At last they're persuaded. 'Well, Dr Brown,' they say, 'it looks like almost everyone wants this. We'll put new legislation in place, and all motorised traffic will be banned from the city centre.' Victory! Victory for people power. We united, and when the authorities saw the weight of public opinion they granted what we wanted.

Not all changes come about that way. But lots do. When there's a sufficient head of steam for an issue, measured by the number of people backing it, policies get changed. Things get done. We know it because we see it happen often enough. The more who want something to happen, the more likely it is to happen.

Our thought processes are programmed by our experiences of that, by how the powers that be are influenced by the weight of numbers. They're not deprogrammed when there's something we want God to do. Yes, we know that God is an authority over us quite different from the rest. His will is meant to be discovered by us, accepted and obeyed. It's not for him to discover our will and do what we want. We realise that. Or we would if we thought about it. But we don't. When we have strong views that something should happen, we approach him with the same attitude as we would anyone else. 'Surely God understands how right my wishes are on this,' we reason. The next stage is easy. 'Surely God will understand even more clearly how right my wishes are if a huge number of others all think the same way.'

But God is never subject to us. It wouldn't matter if the whole world united in one view on something, if that thing was not God's will he wouldn't grant it. We – no matter how many of us there are – never become lord over God. God's will is not determined by man's vote on what should be done.

Lots of people prayed for Karen, but she still died. So many were praying, we thought she should be healed. We were wrong to think like that. To us numbers matter. They persuade people to concede to us. But it's not like that with prayer. However prayer works it isn't by persuading God to concede to his servants. In that sense the number who pray about an issue is irrelevant. Could God have healed Karen? Certainly. Was it his will to heal her? Self-evidently it wasn't. It was our will, but not his. Even if we'd doubled the number of those who prayed for Karen, it still wouldn't have become his will. She still would have died.

Shared prayer matters

So it really makes no difference how many pray for something to happen? I wouldn't go that far. Lots of people praying may not mean God's arm gets twisted, but there are still gains. One: the fellowship of shared prayer matters.

There is strength in bearing each other's burdens, including prayer burdens. You feel loved and supported when you know someone is praying for your problem. Two: others are often better at listening for God's will than the person at the heart of an issue. Often a prayer topic matters so much to me I'm not laying a request before God but telling him the answer. Someone else, not so emotionally involved and therefore not so spiritually deaf, may discern what God has in mind and help me accept it. Three: sometimes those closest to a problem struggle the most with lack of faith. Their anxiety, pain or shock numbs their spiritual life, and it can be hard to pray. Who can say how important it is at those times for others to utter the prayers the wounded or fearful cannot pray?

In the end, though, no matter how many pray, the answer we want may still not come. Whatever the campaign of prayer that's mounted, God's will is never moved to coincide with our prayers. That's how it is.

Suppose we *could* change God's will by getting enough to pray? Would we really want that? I'm not sure we would. It could be an intolerable pressure. What if an answer to prayer didn't come because I'd failed to mobilise enough prayer support? I'd be terrorised by the possibility that just one or two more would have made the difference. Even more intolerable is the thought that I and others were determining what God should do. All I'd need would be enough to agree with me and I could have anything! It's attractive and appalling. Our world wouldn't survive long if people power ruled.

God has spared us from all that by never promising to change his will according to the number who pray the same way. We do neither God nor ourselves any favours by inventing the idea.

10

You must read your Bible every day

Brian Smith had never been the most likely of converts. He wasn't quite a diamond in the rough, but his life was far from polished. A tearaway in his late teens and twenties, he was a well-known acquaintance of the local police. Thankfully most of his misdemeanours were not the kind that make headlines. If he had terrorised anyone, it was probably the parents of the succession of young women he'd dated, none of whom reckoned him much of a prospect as a son-in-law.

Yet it was getting married to Louisa when he was twenty-seven which marked the beginning of the change in him. Louisa brought stability and even discipline into Brian's life, qualities which had never been there before. He settled to his work as a builder's labourer, and even became friendly to his neighbours. The arrival of baby Susan, followed two years later by Peter, added yet another dimension to his life, and did nothing but good for him.

It was Louisa who first showed up at church. When she was a child she'd been dragged to Sunday School. She'd hated it, yet some strands of the gospel she was taught had lodged in her. Now she wanted her children to attend a Sunday School, but she'd bring them, not send them. From the earliest weeks, it was obvious there was something deeper to Louisa's interest than that, and within six months she made a quiet, undramatic commitment of her life to Christ.

Brian had been happy enough for Louisa to come to

church with the children. At that stage he kept well clear of services, but when a work party was organised to do some decorating and gardening around the church building, Brian came along. 'Glad to help,' he said. He was a good worker, and the fringe benefit was getting to know the men of the congregation. They took him bowling, and some weeks later he went with them to watch a football match. Not long after that I looked out at the congregation one Sunday morning to see Louisa with Brian alongside her. That became the new pattern. When we had a special evangelistic service with an appeal at the end, Brian marched to the front. I counselled him myself. He wanted to put the last and most important thing right in his life, to be at peace with God. Would Jesus take someone like him? I assured him he would. Spontaneously and with tears streaming down his face, Brian prayed. The words were stumbling and ungrammatical but utterly sincere as he thanked Jesus for saving him. There was no doubt he knew what he was doing. Afterwards I drew him aside, handed him a brand new Bible in a modern translation, and urged him to read it. He took the Bible a little nervously, but then thanked me profusely.

A week later I visited him with an invitation to a class for new Christians. I noticed the Bible sitting on a shelf, looking untouched. 'Isn't he taking his faith seriously?' I wondered, but out of politeness said nothing. He came to the class which had about six in total. I should have known better, but asked different members of the group to read out the Bible verses that we were studying. When it came to Brian's turn, I gave him the reference, then instantly realised there was a problem. He opened his Bible aimlessly and stared at a page not remotely near the one from which I wanted him to read. Trying to be helpful, and knowing how difficult it is for new converts to learn the geography of the Bible, I reached over, took the book and found the place for him. I waited for Brian to read. There was a long, pregnant silence, and everyone felt uncomfortable. At least a minute later Brian closed his Bible, shrugged his shoulders, and said, 'I'm sorry. I'm not really able to read.' I rescued the situation as best I could, but Brian's acute embarrassment was obvious.

If he felt a failure, I felt even more of one for my naïve assumptions. I had handed Brian a book of 1500 pages, in part written well over two thousand years ago, arising from a culture which was totally alien to his, describing a history completely unknown to him, and told him to get on with learning it all. The most educated of people would have felt daunted. Brian had little education and no proper reading skills. He hadn't a chance. Could I – overaged, overweight, and underfit – run a marathon because someone told me I should? What I'd asked of Brian was equally unreasonable.

Who's reading the Bible?

The more I thought about Brian, the more I wondered how often I'd presumed other new Christians would simply get on with Bible reading. Worse, I started to question how many long-established Christians were really getting to grips with the Bible.

Over a period of time I asked them. Enquiries had to be subtle – not many will admit to their pastor that they're not reading their Bibles. But it seemed people fell into the following categories:

- a few – very few – could say, 'I read it daily, understand it, and benefit from it'
- more fitted the description, 'I read it occasionally, don't understand it too well and don't usually feel it's done me much good, but I know I must read some verses every day'
- many had opted for some form of Bible-reading aid, consisting of a Scripture passage followed by comment, and would admit, 'I don't like reading more than just a

few verses at a time, but the notes which accompany the reading are often helpful'
• a considerable number hinted that their Bible reading took place solely at church services, though some also got their Bibles out for a mid-week home Bible study group. Otherwise it was all too difficult to grasp, and there was never enough time.

Apart from those in the first of these categories, most people carried a substantial guilt complex about Bible reading. They knew they should do more – they ought to read their Bibles properly every day – and they felt bad that they were falling short.

Why Bible reading matters

Bible-reading failure guilt is driven by all we've been taught about the Bible, things which make the Bible hugely important for evangelicals. It's how we know what God is like, for its inspired and (many would say) infallible revelation reveals his character and work perfectly. It's God's word to us, God's law for us, God's explanation of what he has done, is doing and will do with this world. It's also how we get the major part of our guidance. While we may sense God's whisper in our hearts about specific details, the Bible gives us the basic and general outline of how we should live. It shapes the goals we set, defines the standards for our conduct and helps us decide between conflicting priorities.

Sometimes Scripture 'speaks' to us as particular verses seem to leap out and become a very direct word of guidance. A friend of mine had grown close to an attractive young woman. Should he marry her or not? He wasn't sure. Just as he was needing to make a decision, his daily reading brought him to Jeremiah 16:1–2, 'Then the word of the LORD came to me: "You must not marry and have sons or daughters in this place."' He ended the relationship. The Bible can be remarkably topical and relevant!

When the Bible means all this to us, it's inconceivable for Christians not to know it. Bible reading may be tough, but it's not optional. Christians who don't learn their Bibles thoroughly deprive themselves of spiritual food and risk silly or serious heresies.

So, in the past I felt driven to try out many types of daily Bible-reading plans. Most lasted less than a week, but I persevered for a long time with the one which was probably the most demanding. It's credited to Robert Murray M'Cheyne, famous Scottish preacher in the first half of the 1800s. The attraction of his scheme is that it takes you through the whole Bible every year, including twice through the New Testament. The downside is that such an ambitious goal requires about four chapters to be read every day. That's not too bad when the passages are straightforward narrative, but long chunks of Levitical laws or Daniel's visions require masochistic determination. To be fair, M'Cheyne split his readings into almost palatable sections which mixed Old and New Testaments for morning and night. But the scheme still required an iron discipline. Even in the less frenetic times of a past century it could never have been easy. With all the distractions of today – phone calls, TV, friends, dashing here and there to meetings – I found it impossible to sustain. After a couple of weeks I was falling behind. I promised myself I'd read five chapters a day until I caught up. Instead I missed a few more. Reading six or more daily soon became inconceivable, and, when I couldn't keep to the schedule, I found I wasn't motivated to keep to the scheme. I dropped it, leaving myself with a confusing mixture of relief and guilt.

Likewise few today keep up with serious daily Bible-reading plans. Perhaps the ethos of our culture, in which discipline is almost a flaw, makes it harder than ever to stick with anything too demanding. So Bible reading becomes patchy. At best many snatch a couple of verses over breakfast, perhaps with some 'daily insight' to give them a thought to take into the day. That eases their consciences about daily Bible reading, and gets them off the hook when the preacher lays into the congregation about not knowing the Bible.

Is daily reading obligatory?

Why, then, do we think we must read the Bible every day? Who said we should?

The following points are not frequently made.

1. The Bible contains no command for Christians to read its pages every day. In a sense, of course, it can't say that, for its writers were usually unconscious that they were putting down anything which would be read by generations to come. They were aware only of writing for an immediate readership and, even then, attempted to address only specific issues. Nevertheless, if God had considered it vital, he could have inspired them to write in an appropriate command about daily Scripture reading. But he didn't. We look to Scripture as our authority for matters of faith and practice, and the Bible doesn't teach that it should be read daily.

2. The first Christians did not read the Bible daily. For Jewish converts, the Old Testament was well known, the core of the education they received as children and the law by which their lives were governed. Large portions of Scripture were memorised, and they heard it read publicly during synagogue or temple worship. But since the average Jewish family didn't own scrolls of its own, no one could get up each morning and do a daily reading. Non-Jewish converts had even less in the way of Scriptures. One of the big disputes of the New Testament was how much a Greek or Roman who believed in Jesus had to take Judaism on board as well. The general conclusion was that he or she didn't. So the vast majority of Gentile believers didn't start

learning the Old Testament, nor, in the first couple of centuries, did they have a New Testament. The letters and gospels were being written through the first century, and began to circulate around the churches. But, though many manuscript copies came into being, the average Christian didn't own a personal collection. Besides, it wasn't until the end of the second century that the New Testament canon (the list of authorised books) was generally accepted, and not until the second half of the fourth century that it was finalised. Even after that, personal daily Bible reading couldn't happen on a wide scale. It became a realistic option for most believers only after the invention of the printing press, the liberalising of attitudes to ownership of the Bible and an improvement in literacy rates. That puts us well into recent history. Reading part of the Bible every day is a comparatively modern phenomenon.

3. The Bible is not suitable to be read daily, at least not in bite-sized morsels. Only a few short sections of Scripture, like the Psalms or Proverbs, can legitimately be taken individually. Most is written in long flowing passages, with carefully constructed building blocks of narrative or logic. Their writers meant them to be read as a whole or at least in large chunks. When Paul dictated his letters, he didn't intend anyone to take two or three verses, analyse the nuances of each word and draw lessons for life from them. Such a method – especially when verses are lifted out of context – almost guarantees distortion of Paul's meaning. One of my happiest memories from early years as a Christian was reading Romans 1 to 8 in a modern translation without stopping. For the first time I grasped the thrust of Paul's argument, understood his logic, and learned new things about the completeness of salvation through Christ. Ordinary mortals will never read the whole of Jeremiah or Revelation at a sitting, but an understanding of what these books are really about

requires significant quantities to be read at a time. Daily portion reading is a bad way to get to know the Bible.

4. Most people do not have a sufficiently high literary, academic and theological standard to cope with large amounts of daily Bible reading. Literacy surveys report that many never read any book after they leave school. At best they glance at tabloid newspapers and some magazines. The complex vocabulary of most Bible translations, plus the sheer volume of words, is beyond them. Even if they can break through the language barrier, understanding the meaning of what's written in the Bible is very difficult especially for those new to it. We don't give infants at school the same course book as those in post-graduate education at university. Yet new-born Christians – babes in Christ – are told to learn from the book which still taxes those who have been believers for decades. It's not that anything should be withheld from the young Christian, but most gain little from raw, unguided exposure to the Bible. Such exposure is counter-productive, for the majority simply give up serious attempts at learning after a short time.

Conclusions

Let me sharpen up some conclusions from these points.

First, God does not require us to read his Bible daily. It is not commanded in Scripture that we should, nor was it required of the first converts. The guilt we feel when we miss our reading is man-induced.

Second, reading tiny portions of the Bible daily may be the worst way of achieving the real goal. What is the point of Bible reading? What are we trying to do? Do we think we're in good spiritual health when we've read a portion? We're not. If we're not grasping what it means the activity is as worthless as any other empty ritual. Our knowledge of God isn't enlarged; our understanding of his purposes with us hasn't grown; our awareness of his will for our lives hasn't altered. The real goal is to know the Bible and be changed by it. Usually that can't be done by a daily three-verse 'Scripture bite'. Mostly the Bible needs to be read at length, and then thought through carefully, so a major section read every second or third day is far better. Anything less may actually hinder us achieving our goal.

Third, the demand for daily Bible reading reduces many to unhelpful and almost dangerous habits. They're not good at reading, and don't have advanced levels of theological understanding, so if they have to read their Bibles every day, all they can manage is a biblical snack. They read less than half a dozen verses, or a collection of verses in their *Daily Light*, or they check the card in their 'Promise Box', or look at the text in the daily newspaper or on their calendar. Those isolated texts can take on inordinate importance and all too easily become a Scriptural horoscope. My friend's decision not to marry is uncomfortably close to an example of that. Another person decided not to have a necessary operation because that morning's verse had been 'I am the LORD, who heals you' (Exod. 15:26). Lifting a few words out of their original contexts like this misses the whole counsel of Scripture. The person who looks at a great painting from only two inches' distance will know a lot about a tiny area, and may think it stunning, but unless he takes a step back to see the whole canvas he'll never grasp what the picture is about. Today's Church is breeding people who are fascinated with particularly stunning texts but have little idea of the big picture which the Bible portrays of God and his work. The insistence on reading a daily Bible portion is partly responsible for that.

From obligation to freedom

One of the hardest things for evangelicals to do is shake off the sense of obligation to read the Bible every day. There's something of the Pharisee in all of us, a part that likes to have rigidly defined rules. It makes things simple. If reading at least a little of the Bible every day pleases God, then we know how to be good Christians. Read some Scripture and God is happy with you. Easy. Even if we learn little, we'll do it. However, because Pharisaism doesn't bring fulfilment, the rot soon sets in. The daily portion becomes a chore, one which degenerates into getting through the reading as quickly as possible. But it's hard to let go. We are prisoners to an unsatisfactory and unsatisfying method of reading the Bible.

Responsible freedom is what we need. What does that involve?

First, it means we take seriously what the Bible says about itself. 'Men spoke from God as they were carried along by the Holy Spirit,' is the verdict of the New Testament about the Old (2 Pet. 1:21). So, it's God's word. We can ignore most people in this world, but we can't ignore God. If he's spoken we must listen. And when we do, our lives get straightened out by the Bible: 'All Scripture is God-breathed and is useful for teaching, rebuking, correcting and training in righteousness, so that the man of God may be thoroughly equipped for every good work' (2 Tim. 3:16–17). In short, if we are to know and serve God rightly, the Bible will tell us how.

Second, we're going to have to know it. Knowing the Bible is not mere memorisation, like the chemistry or mathematics student who learns formulae off by heart but has no idea what they mean. If we are to be 'corrected and trained in righteousness' we must understand about God and understand his will for us. How we learn these from the Bible will vary. What the new convert can grasp, reading the Bible for the first time, is different from what the Christian of many decades will absorb. They may need to use different translations, tackle different amounts at one time and read at different frequencies. The point for both is to learn and apply what the Bible has to say.

I don't read the Bible every day, but neither do I read

it just when I'm in the mood. I set aside time deliberately, and read a logical amount. At the time of writing this, I'm progressing through 2 Chronicles. Usually I read the whole account of a particular king, whether that's half a chapter or three chapters. When I'm finished, I sit and think. What has that passage told me about God, human nature, strengths and weaknesses, or how I should live my life? That reflection time can be as long as the Bible reading. But that's okay, for the point is to learn, not merely to read. When I open my Bible next – which could be the following day but may not be – I remember what I learned last and I can build on it. So I grow spiritually. That's what matters, not complying with a man-made ritual of getting through a few verses of the Bible every day.

The Brian Smiths of this world are not helped by being told they must read the Bible daily. At worst, the obligation becomes the first nail in their coffin of failure. Hammer in enough nails and they become imprisoned in that coffin. They die spiritually, feeling they'll never be good enough to be real Christians. At best, the Brian Smiths grit their teeth and stagger through a few verses every day. They believe they're pleasing God by their daily readings, not realising their tiny portions of Scripture provide only edited highlights of the whole truth God has for them.

If they'd let go of the ritual and relax in Bible reading, they'd find there's a wonderful book waiting to be learned in a more sensible way, one which will open their eyes more to God, his love, his world, and to their importance to him.

11

God wants you happy

'God is even more interested in your happiness than you are!' The speaker smiled broadly, and so did his audience. Several hundred Levi-clad teens were lapping up reassurances that they could trust God. 'You don't need to be afraid of his will,' they were told, 'for God wants you happy.'

I was quite a few years older than the rest, supposedly a bit more mature and knowledgeable, but I'd never heard that said before. I'd always known that deep down I'd be satisfied if I was in the will of God, and that I ought to feel pleased and privileged to serve him. But doing what God wanted was hard. I'd given up a good career and income, and was trying to get through university while supporting a young family. Obedience was coming at a price, and serving God didn't always feel good. But God wanted me happy. I liked that. I was impressed.

I stayed impressed for a long time. That speaker's words nipped in the bud the evangelical nonsense which says that if you enjoy something it can't possibly be God's will. I was never going to give up playing golf or eating cream cakes, but I might have felt guilty about them. Now I knew that God wanted me happy I could shed my guilt. And when big decisions came, my right to happiness could become the guiding principle. If God's will would make me happy, anything I didn't like could be rejected.

It took a friend, a school-teacher, to make me rethink. Standing tall and broad, this was not one of those teachers a little child with a skinned knee would run to for a healing cuddle. The looks summed up the character: biceps bulging, chin set square, voice rasping, looking as though a horse had been eaten for breakfast. Any man would have been proud of the macho image, but this was Wilma, making a unique contribution to denying the existence of a fairer sex.

She was in her early thirties, and on the hunt for a man. She made no great secret of that, which at least gave the targets of her matrimonial ambitions time to scurry for cover. One day I risked suggesting to Wilma that God might not mean everyone to marry. I knew she believed a Christian should marry only another Christian, so, I argued, a two to one ratio of women to men in church made marriage impossible for everyone unless we approved polygamy. Wilma fixed me with one of her fiercest looks. 'I understand,' she said with all the grace of a pit bull terrier, 'but God does not mean *me* to be single, because he knows that wouldn't make me happy.' That was it. She saw no flaw in her logic: only marriage would make her happy, therefore God must want her married.

So, does God really organise his will for us around our happiness? Why are we so convinced God wants us happy?

Accentuating the positive

The answer to that starts with the way evangelism is done. For decades evangelists have known that religion and the Church are big turn-offs for non-Christians. Church services are reckoned dull and boring. Christian belief is considered redundant in a fast-changing world. Who wants outmoded customs? Who cares about old morals that take the fun out of life? Who's interested in spiritual pie in the sky when you die when there's so much to be doing while you're alive? Those assessments of Christianity aren't fair, but they're how people see our faith. Tell someone, 'We had a great prayer meeting last night.' Does he respond with, 'Wow! Can I come next week?' Not likely. He looks at you as a weird eccentric who doesn't belong in the real world. Prayer meetings are not considered thrill-a-minute experiences, nor is door-to-door visitation, nor church committees, nor lengthy sermons. Today's secular generation does not want to be preached at. Nor is it motivated to sing from musty hymn books in dingy buildings, seated on old wooden benches, listening as someone whose voice lost its tunefulness thirty years ago gives a 'rendering', the evening rounded off with stewed tea served from giant tea-pots. Others are not like us, who consider this experience such a privilege that we pay for it by giving an offering, sometimes being told later we didn't contribute enough. This is not the world's idea of fun. Evangelists, astute people that they are, have noticed that. Christianity has an image problem.

The answer has been to do what every salesman does, accentuate the positive and ignore the negative of what's on offer. So, when I was a teenage consumer of evangelistic rallies, I was promised fabulous benefits if I would come to Christ. I would be free instantaneously of guilt, flooded with inner peace, feel close to God, find a new meaning to life, get God's strength for every day, rise above all my problems and have complete fulfilment. Above all, I'd be happy. In fact, coming to Christ was the only way to real happiness. The world's pleasures were fleeting, but true joy would be found if only I pledged myself to Jesus. I would have a lifetime – no, more than that, an eternity – of bliss if only I'd become a Christian. Wasn't it the best of all bargains?

It certainly was. Many like me bought that package, and entered Christianity assured of peace and joy. One of the reasons Wilma reckoned she was entitled to happiness was because it had been part of the deal between her and God when she first became a Christian.

Knowing God makes you feel good

The evangelistic salesman's starter pack of happiness has been reinforced week by week by preachers. Opening prayers, after thanking God for creation and Christ, often go on to gratitude for 'the satisfaction and blessings we have received, for helping us to find purpose and fulfilment, joy and happiness . . .' God is praised for making life so much better. Later comes the sermon. Who does the preacher say is the miserable person in this world? The sinner who doesn't know God. Who is the happy person? The forgiven, renewed believer into whose lap God wants to pour all good things. Some gild that particular lily to the extent of promising health and wealth as well as happiness. Those who don't go that far still leave the Christian assured of a great life by knowing God and doing God's will. Constantly the message is drummed in: being a Christian and serving God will make you feel good.

That's also the subtle and unsubtle message of Christian testimonies. Colin is asked to share his story. 'Before I was a Christian,' he tells his audience, 'I was a terrible person. At work I was driven by ambition, and though I got promotion after promotion, it felt empty. My personal life was a mess. I had a string of girlfriends, but none of the relationships ever lasted. I turned to drink to drown my sorrows, but it was escapism. I cried myself to sleep at night, and woke with a headache next morning. Was this all there was to life? I was depressed, and wondered if it was worth going on living. Then I met someone who seemed to have an extra dimension to his personality. Day by day I watched him. Nothing ever seemed to get him down – he was always happy. So I asked him what made his life different. He told me it was Jesus. At first I laughed, but one day he asked me to go to a Christian meeting with him. I heard the speaker say that Jesus could take all my sins away and give me a brand new life. That night I gave my heart to the Lord. Since then all my problems have gone, and I have a joy inside that never leaves me. God has given me a beautiful wife, a great career and a new attitude.

He answers my prayers, helps me through hard times and makes life worth living. I'm content – more than that – I'm on top of the world! I wake up every morning bursting with energy. I can't wait to see what the Lord will bring into my life that day. The greatest thing that ever happened to me is meeting Jesus. He's filled my life with overflowing joy, and given me a happiness the non-Christian can never know.'

Good for Colin. And I have heard fifty different variations of that testimony. They all follow the same pattern: life was miserable before conversion but it's been marvellous since. The consistent message the listener gets is that becoming a Christian will make you happy.

'Happy I shall be'

More than prayers, more than sermons, more than testimonies, it's the hymns and songs which tell us our Christian commitment is an investment in happiness. And the conditioning starts young:

I've got the joy, joy, joy, joy down in my heart
  down in my heart
  down in my heart
I've got the joy, joy, joy, joy down in my heart
Down in my heart to stay

I'm H-A-P-P-Y
I'm H-A-P-P-Y
I know I am, I'm sure I am,
I'm H-A-P-P-Y

I'm in-right, out-right, up-right, down-right happy all
  the time
I'm in-right, out-right, up-right, down-right happy all
  the time
Since Jesus Christ came in, and washed away my sin
I'm in-right, out-right, up-right, down-right happy all
  the time

For generations, children in Christian meetings have sung of how being a Christian makes them feel full of joy. Climbing sunshine mountain makes our faces glow. God supplies never-ending happiness.

Nineteenth-century hymn writers composed their works against a social background of hard realities like high rates of infant mortality, but used them to contrast the happiness children could know if they gave their lives to Jesus. Here's an anonymous example:

> *I'm not too young to sin,*
> *I'm not too young to die,*
> *I'm not too little to begin*
> *A life of faith and joy.*

Realism, though, has never been allowed to intrude too much. Most hymn writers kept their sentiments simple and appealing, like this example from Fanny Crosby:

> *If I come to Jesus,*
> *He will make me glad;*
> *He will give me pleasure*
> *When my heart is sad.*
>
> *If I come to Jesus,*
> *Happy I shall be,*
> *He is gently calling*
> *Little ones like me.*

What does it do to young minds fed a steady diet of those songs? What kind of theology is imbued? It's one which tells them that being a Christian and being happy are inextricably linked.

As children get older, the message doesn't change.

> *There's a psalm of praise filling all my days,*
> *Since to Jesus my heart did bow;*
> *O what melody! Glorious harmony!*
> *Life is wonderful now:*

> *Life is wonderful, Yes, it's wonderful!*
> *Life is wonderful now to me!*
> *I let Jesus in, He changed ev'rything,*
> *Life is wonderful now!*
> *Since His blessings came into my heart,*
> *Joy unspeakable fills every part,*
> *And I want to live for my Lord;*
> *Life is wonderful now!*

It may have a high cringe factor, but not so long ago (i.e. in my time) that was one of the most popular songs among youth groups. Its second verse is no less positive.

> *All is happiness, gone is my distress,*
> *Peace and vict'ry He does endow;*
> *Since my Saviour came, I can't be the same;*
> *Life is wonderful now:*

Musical catechising doesn't stop when you grow up. Adult choruses, old and new, are no less rapturous in their message:

> *Joy, joy my heart is full of joy;*
> *Joy, joy my heart is full of joy;*
> > *My Saviour dear*
> > *Is ever near;*
> *That's the reason why my heart is full of joy.*

Happiness in our hearts, peace in our souls, and victory in our lives are confident promises in modern worship songs. Troubles disappear, joy is without limit, we march from triumph to triumph over Satan and sin. Christianity is certainly presented as a desirable package!

Of course the Psalms often say joy comes from knowing and serving God, and no one wants to sing about having a hard time. But, equally, no one should underestimate the impact of this constant intake of happiness teaching. The association between being a Christian and being happy is so close that it's assumed that if the first is there the second will be also.

A right to be happy

That assumption – a Christian will be happy – thrives in today's hedonistic, self-centred culture. 'I love me and want me to be happy' mentality is rife. I discovered that as a pastor the first time I tried to mend a broken marriage. A young couple – aged no more than mid-twenties – had split up after about three years.

'Diane just walked out,' Jack told me, 'and I don't know why.'

When I met with Diane I asked, 'Why did you leave Jack? Was he being unfaithful, cruel, uncaring?'

'No, nothing like that,' she replied. 'I simply wasn't happy. And I have a right to be happy.'

That was it. There was no other reason – no fights, no third party – just less than a full quota of happiness. For the sake of her right to happiness, Diane had jettisoned her marriage.

Christians are not immune from thinking like that. Of course, neither to themselves nor to others would Christians want to appear so blatantly selfish. Therefore, instead of saying, 'I have a right to be happy,' the Christian says, 'God wants me happy.' It's still hedonism – devotion to pleasure – but spiritual hedonism, believing God's purpose is to give me pleasure. The world may soon want 'the right to happiness' to appear on a citizens' charter. Christians seem to have decided 'the right to happiness' is already on God's charter. Hence we have people like Wilma who was so sure God wanted her happy that it had to be his will for her to get married.

What's wrong with all this? What's bad about the salesman approach to evangelism, and the positive emphasis in the prayers and preaching, the testimonies and the songs? None of them tells outright lies. Why not boast that there's

joy in knowing God and being in his family? The Bible has
hundreds of statements like that. What's wrong with saying
that God wants his children to be happy? A God of love is
bound to care about the well-being of his people.

Not all of those things are wrong. There is great joy in
knowing God, and he certainly cares for his children. But
such simple truths do not amount to the simplistic and
unbiblical statement that God wants me happy.

Doing without what we want

First, Jesus did not teach self-indulgence but self-sacrifice.
He constantly warned those who followed him what the
terms of discipleship were.

> Then he said to them all: 'If anyone would come after
> me, he must deny himself and take up his cross daily and
> follow me. For whoever wants to save his life will lose it,
> but whoever loses his life for me will save it. What good
> is it for a man to gain the whole world, and yet lose or
> forfeit his very self? If anyone is ashamed of me and my
> words, the Son of Man will be ashamed of him when he
> comes in his glory and in the glory of the Father and of
> the holy angels.' (Luke 9:23–6)

Quite clearly 'anyone' who would follow Jesus 'must deny
himself'. Familiarity with those words has blunted them:
far from automatically being given everything they want to
keep them happy, Christians will often have to do without
the things they want. When there's a clash between the will
of God and the will of the Christian, the will of God *must*
prevail.

Jesus taught that with great force. He used the metaphor
of taking up the cross to describe what it was like to be a
disciple. Those who heard him would have drawn in their
breath sharply. They'd seen Roman soldiers come to a
village, arrest a man and take him off for crucifixion,

perhaps carrying his cross to the execution site. No one ever came back. To carry the cross was to be on a one-way journey to death. In its context, Jesus's metaphor is about dying to self-will. Daily the Christian lays down his goals, his ambitions, his desires, his life. If he won't – if he wants to 'save his life' – Jesus says he'll be lost for ever. He may gain all this world offers, but nothing of what Jesus offers. Anyone ashamed of Jesus and his teaching will be rejected at Jesus's return. That's strong language but what it means to be a Christian. Self-sacrifice is fundamental to discipleship, without the tiniest space for self-indulgence. The idea that God's will can be reshaped to coincide with ours is not only a nonsense, it's a reversal of what Jesus taught. It is anathema to the gospel.

That teaching was not a freak, eccentric and over-enthusiastic remark from Jesus. It was a frequent theme of his, perhaps because many followed him for dubious motives. Jesus often met their needs, perhaps a meal, perhaps healing for their illness. But he never wanted people to think they could enter Christianity for the superficial things they could get from it. 'Large crowds were travelling with Jesus, and turning to them he said: "If anyone comes to me and does not hate his father and mother, his wife and children, his brothers and sisters – yes, even his own life – he cannot be my disciple. And anyone who does not carry his cross and follow me cannot be my disciple"' (Luke 14:25–7). There's nothing wrong with fathers, mothers, wives, children, brothers, sisters, nor with anyone's own life. These are all good things. But Jesus's 'hate' language about them was his way of stressing that they must be at least second to him. And again he spoke about the cross – his followers must die to their own desires. Without that, he said, a person 'cannot be my disciple'. A little later he told them, 'In the same way, any of you who does not give up everything he has cannot be my disciple' (Luke 14:33). Suffering and sacrifice are part of normal Christianity.

Simplistic ideas of personal happiness don't fit with this. Language of the cross is always language of pain. There may be a deep inner peace in doing God's will, no matter how hard, but that's another matter. What Jesus taught was that a Christian cannot make a goal of self-happiness, self-pleasure, self-will. Following Jesus requires death to self's priorities.

'You will have trouble'

Second, the Bible teaches that being a Christian will be hard, not easy. The Christian may be heading for peaceful celestial shores, but it's on a battleship under fire, not a cruise liner.

'In this world you will have trouble,' warned Jesus (John 16:33). He told his disciples that people would insult them, persecute them and falsely accuse them of evil (Matt. 5:11). He warned that they would be arrested and flogged (Matt. 10:17). Even family members would betray them – a brother would hand over his brother, a father his child, children their parents – even though the betrayal would lead to their death. Far from being liked for standing up for what is right and good, they would be hated by everyone for being Christians (Matt. 10:21–2; 24:9). Just as he had been called the devil, so they would be accused similarly (Matt. 10:24–5). On the whole, Jesus expected his disciples to be treated the same as him. 'Remember the words I spoke to you: "No servant is greater than his master." If they persecuted me, they will persecute you also' (John 15:20).

From the earliest days of the Church, Jesus's disciples found his words fulfilled. It's only a slight exaggeration to say the pages of Acts flow with Christian blood. Peter and John are jailed and threatened (Acts 4). Soon all the apostles are flogged (Acts 5), Stephen dies under a hail of stones (Acts 7), and Christians flee their homes as persecution spreads (Acts 8). Paul, not long a believer, faces the first of many attempts on his life (Acts 9). James is executed, and Peter escapes the same fate only because he's led out of jail by an angel (Acts 12). And on it goes like that through the rest of Acts. It was warfare, and it was tough. 'Endure hardship with us like a good soldier of Christ Jesus,' Timothy is told (2 Tim. 2:3). That's putting it mildly. The Christian army had no sinecures, no posts out of the firing line and no way to opt out before the war was over.

Neither Jesus nor the writers of the New Testament promised Christians an easy time, and certainly not lives of undiluted bliss. They would sail through stormy waters, not glide serenely over a mill pond; they would be hurt by enemy fire, not become spiritual supermen immune from harm; they would often be stopped short of their goals, not victorious in every conflict. In other words, being a Christian would be really hard. Pain might outweigh pleasure. Privation might outweigh comfort. In respect of anything of this world, disciples might be more victims than victors, and happiness is not a natural product of that.

Distress and despair

Third, biblical examples abound of people who struggled, and felt the pain of it. It was not the happiest moment of Jeremiah's life when his enemies took such a dislike to his prophesying that they shoved him down a well (Jer. 38:6). The good news was it happened in the dry season and there was only mud at the bottom. The bad news was that that meant a slow lingering death from exposure and starvation rather than a comparatively quick drowning. Jeremiah's thoughts aren't recorded, but it's as well he didn't believe in a right to personal happiness, or he'd have gone through a severe crisis of faith while down the well.

And there are many more instances when God's servants were none too thrilled with life. Jacob was robbed of seven years, trapped into forced labour for his father-in-law. Naomi suffered the loss of her husband and two sons. Samson had his eyes gouged out and lived his last days wearing shackles, grinding grain in a Philistine prison. Job's sons and daughters met a violent death and he suffered agony from sores over his whole body. Elijah's victory on Mount Carmel was short-lived for him personally as Queen Jezebel's threats so terrified him he fled into the desert and prayed to be allowed to die. As we've seen, Stephen and James died cruel deaths. John was exiled to the tiny island of Patmos. None of these people were happy about those experiences.

Perhaps the most honest admission that at times he felt miserable comes from Paul, and especially in 2 Corinthians where he describes his 'troubles' (1:4), 'sufferings' (1:6) and 'hardships' (1:8). They left him feeling 'distressed' (1:6), 'under great pressure, far beyond our ability to endure, so that we despaired even of life' (1:8). Later Paul lists what he's been through. There's deep emotion in his words.

> Are they servants of Christ? (I am out of my mind to talk like this.) I am more. I have worked much harder, been in prison more frequently, been flogged more severely, and been exposed to death again and again. Five times I received from the Jews the forty lashes minus one. Three times I was beaten with rods, once I was stoned, three times I was shipwrecked, I spent a night and a day in the open sea, I have been constantly on the move. I have been in danger from rivers, in danger from bandits, in danger from my own countrymen, in danger from Gentiles; in danger in the city, in danger in the country, in danger at sea; and in danger from false brothers. I have laboured and toiled and have often gone without sleep; I have known hunger and thirst and have often gone without food; I have been cold and naked. Besides everything else, I face daily the pressure of my concern for all the churches. Who is weak, and I do not feel weak? Who is led into sin, and I do not inwardly burn? (2 Cor. 11:23–9)

I wonder how many times during that catalogue of pain and disaster words like *Life is wonderful, Yes, it's wonderful! Life is wonderful now to me!* sprang to his lips? Was that how he felt when he was flogged? As the stones rained down on his head, drawing blood and making him wonder if he was about to die, did he feel good? When his clothes were stripped from him and he was left naked, shivering and hungry, was he thinking about his right to be happy?

He *was* grateful to God. Had he stayed a Pharisee he would have had many advantages in this world but none he could have taken to the next. Those old things that once he thought so valuable he now counted as 'rubbish' compared to having Christ (Phil. 3:8). It was worth losing everything else to gain Jesus. But, true though that was, it didn't make Paul's life easy, or fun, or filled with ordinary happiness. Paul's life *wasn't* easy. He kept going because of God's power and the hope of what lay ahead ultimately. 'If the earthly tent we live in is destroyed, we have a building from God, an eternal house in heaven, not built by human hands. Meanwhile we groan, longing to be clothed with our heavenly dwelling . . .' (2 Cor. 5:1–2)

God's people don't always walk around smiling. Often they go through terrible experiences, and they don't feel good about them.

The primary goal

Fourth, those who promote happiness theology have confused primary goals and secondary gains.

Plenty of non-Christians will answer the question 'What do you want from life?' with 'I want to be happy', but that's not Christian thinking. We don't exist to be happy. Being happy is not the purpose of our lives. However, at the risk of setting a riddle, Christians will find happiness providing they don't pursue it.

An illustration may explain the mystery. Suppose my goal is to have a well-ordered garden, with weeds out, grass trimmed and flowers and vegetables planted. And suppose I slave away day after day, and get all that done. My garden is now looking great. Do I feel happy? I certainly do. I have enormous pleasure and satisfaction. Why? Because I did something I like? No, I don't like gardening. Gardening is time-consuming and backbreaking, and definitely not fun. If I wanted fun I'd play golf, or watch a film, or raid the fridge. So why am I happy? Simply because I feel a deep inner satisfaction when my garden is at its best. When the work's been done well, and everything's neat and colourful and my home-grown vegetables are in the dinner pot, I feel pleased.

What was the priority? Not happiness. I wouldn't have done gardening if I was after that. The priority was the well-ordered garden, and the by-product of that was pleasure.

From that illustration come two points:

1. If happiness was my primary goal I'd jettison many of the things discipleship requires. Christians have a rough time in this world. The cost of following Jesus is high.

2. Yet I'm happy as a Christian. I'm not chasing happiness but I'm finding it because it's a spin-off from what is the actual primary goal of my life.

What is that goal? What does God want for me above all else? That's a big question, but a simple answer is that he wants me holy. He wants me back to his original purpose for his creation: someone who reflects his image, who is in fellowship with him, who serves him in this world. That's the primary goal. And the secondary gain is that when I live like that I'm fulfilled. Life is good.

Being a Christian *is* good. It's tough, because the world gives us a hard time, and there are things we'd like which we have to sacrifice. But Christians have always reckoned that what's lost is of insignificant value compared to what's gained in Christ. We have infinitely precious gifts like forgiveness, inner peace, hope, assurance, power, eternal life. God has become a loving Father. He shows mercy over the past, gives strength for the present, and promises companionship right into a glorious future. Knowing all that, Christians rejoice and feel thankful. In other words, joy is a *consequence* of being right with God. It's the secondary, almost unsought blessing. 'I have set the LORD always before me. Because he is at my right hand, I shall not be shaken. *Therefore* my heart is glad and my tongue rejoices . . .' (Psalm 16:8–9 – the italics are mine).

The problem with saying 'God wants me happy' is not so much the error as the emphasis of the statement. Especially in the ears of the self-centred, the words suggest that what matters most is our personal happiness, that God's goal is to make us feel good. We then set aside everything that doesn't make us feel good, anything that's difficult, anything that hurts, anything that doesn't square with our own desires. It can't be from God, we tell ourselves, because it doesn't make me happy. Thus we edit or censor the will of God until it fits with our definition of happiness.

That prioritising of happiness confuses what's secondary with what's primary. Happiness isn't the goal of our Christian faith, but holiness is. True happiness is a derivative of holiness: living in a right relationship with God.

Our ultimate good

In what sense, then, does God want us happy? He wants it like a doctor wants his patient happy, and that is with real health. The patient enjoys lazing around on a couch; the doctor tells him to get out and jog. The patient wants to eat fried food and cream buns; the doctor tells him to follow a diet low in calories and high in carbohydrates, with lots of fibre and fresh vegetables. The patient likes to smoke and drink; the doctor tells him to cut out the former and moderate the latter. Doesn't the doctor care about the patient's happiness? Yes, he cares so much for his patient's happiness he won't let him exchange his long-term health and well-being for a few fleeting short-term pleasures. He'll guard him from foolish self-indulgence which will ultimately hurt him. He'll guide him towards self-discipline, exercise and sacrifice which will ultimately benefit him. If the patient trusts his doctor, he'll do what he says, knowing deep in his heart that the cost of following his physician's advice is worth it. It will be for his real good.

Likewise, God cares for his people far beyond their superficial whims. He requires discipline from us, often making us give up things we'd like, not because he's a killjoy or likes depriving us, but because he wants our long-term good. If he takes anything away it's only because it doesn't produce that ultimate good in our lives. If he brings something in, even something hard and costly, it's only because it helps us find that ultimate good.

Does God want us happy? God wants us happy so much that he won't let us grab for superficial pleasures. He takes us down the road of the cross, through pain and sacrifice, to an eternal happiness and joy alongside which this world's pleasures are like the dullest glow of the poorest torch beside the overwhelming blaze of the mid-day sun.

12

The heart of church life is the prayer meeting

'And first in the intermediate section for colour slides is the picture "Twelfth Dog" by member 365.' A slight flush of pride and embarrassment could have been the only hint to the large crowd that I was that month's winner in the photographic society's regular competition. A house move had freed me from old obligations, and we hadn't been settled long enough to pick up new ones. So, for once in my manic Christian life, I had time for a hobby. From when I was a boy I'd taken pictures, and photography would have been my profession if my parents hadn't talked me out of it. That was one of the best pieces of guidance they ever gave me, but the love of cameras and taking photos never left.

Belonging to an active and prestigious photographic society was a real joy for me. I went to the lectures almost every week, entranced by the superb and stunning camera work of top photographers. My competitive spirit was fulfilled by the once-a-month competitions in which members' work was assessed. I was progressing through their league system, and it was near certain that I'd be promoted to the advanced section at the end of the season.

I never got that promotion. It wasn't because I didn't take any more good pictures. It was because the church we'd joined got tough about attending the prayer meeting.

The photographic society met on a Wednesday night; the church prayer meeting was also on a Wednesday night.

Until then I hadn't felt under any obligation to meet with a dozen to twenty others for prayer. But gradually I was getting known. I'd preached one Sunday, and the members knew I was training for the ministry. Surely someone like that would be at the prayer meeting? Shouldn't everyone be there? The pastor thought so. There were good things happening in the church: several being converted; numbers increasing; serious talk of planting a daughter congregation. With a mixture of anger, passion and warning he told us one Sunday: 'If this church does not start turning out in force to the prayer meeting, the blessing will stop.'

So that was the end of the photographic society. Being a conscientious fellow with occasional bursts of spirituality, and certainly with no wish to be the one to cause the blessing to stop, I had to choose to be at the prayer meeting.

Many times and in many places since then I've been told that the church prayer meeting is crucial. 'The spiritual life of a congregation can be measured by the number attending the prayer meeting.' Or, 'The number praying together is the barometer of spiritual health.'

Those sayings are common, but they pale into insignificance compared to the general statement, 'Pastor, there's not enough corporate prayer in this church.' I'd be indecently wealthy if I had a tenner for every time I've heard that. Last time it was said, I had the impertinence to ask the young man who'd given me the rebuke whether he could conceive that our church or any church would ever have *enough* prayer. The question made him think. It had never occurred to him that a church could pray enough. Finally he said, 'No, I don't think we could ever pray enough.' I'd guessed he would say that. His passion that corporate prayer is the spiritual powerhouse of the church generates an insatiable appetite for communal prayer.

He, and the vast numbers who share his views, see clear reasons why prayer meetings should be prioritised.

'Where two or three . . .'

Corporate prayer has special power. Put fifty people together to pray and there's more power than asking the same fifty to pray about the same issues independently.

Why that should be is hard to define, but may have to do with a special presence of Christ. Jesus seemed to promise it. 'Where two or three come together in my name, there am I with them' (Matt. 18:20). Not infrequently those words are quoted at the start of a prayer meeting to allow everyone to feel better about the small turnout. Nevertheless, here is a clear statement that Jesus is with his people when they gather in his name. Is he not with them individually all the time? Yes, he is. His final words, 'Surely I am with you always, to the very end of the age' (Matt. 28:20), have always been accepted as true for every Christian personally. Christ never leaves us. Yet he made a specific pledge to be with his people when even two or three gathered in his name. That makes prayer meetings special. It's as if we get extra attention when we all turn up to talk to him together.

Prayer priority

Prayer was the number one activity of the Church even before it was officially the Church. Prior to Pentecost, the Christians met continually for prayer. They had been through extreme experiences. Emotions had swung wildly from the trauma of the cross to the confusion and ecstasy of the resurrection. Teaching on the kingdom of God had been followed by commissioning to carry on Christ's work. Then he'd disappeared at his ascension. After all that they could have been excused taking a little time off to assimilate what had happened. But time off wasn't on their minds. 'They all joined together constantly in prayer, along with the women and Mary the mother of Jesus, and with his brothers' (Acts 1:14).

If we needed evidence of how highly they ranked

corporate prayer, this is it. They knew how weak and vulnerable they were, and they knew the enormity of the task ahead of them. Therefore, rather than do anything else, they prayed.

They went on praying together

If they prayed pre-Pentecost, they prayed at least as much post-Pentecost. Acts 2:42 seems to describe the early Church pattern: 'They devoted themselves to the apostles' teaching and to the fellowship, to the breaking of bread and to prayer.' Those words imply a lot of commitment. 'See that, pastor,' I'm told. 'They didn't merely pray, they *devoted* themselves to prayer.' Prayer was serious business.

Therefore they prayed together in times of crisis. Peter and John got into trouble for preaching that Jesus was raised from the dead. They were thrown in jail overnight and next morning made to give account of themselves before the Jewish authorities. They spoke well, which was great for the gospel but less wonderful for their personal survival. They were threatened, and left in no doubt what would happen if they carried on preaching. How did they and the other Christians respond to intimidation? 'On their release, Peter and John went back to their own people and reported all that the chief priests and elders had said to them. When they heard this, they raised their voices together in prayer to God' (Acts 4:23–4). They didn't run away, or take arms; they prayed. And God set his seal it: 'After they prayed, the place where they were meeting was shaken. And they were all filled with the Holy Spirit and spoke the word of God boldly' (Acts 4:31).

When in danger they prayed together, and God gave them strength to go on.

They reacted the same way later when there was more persecution. King Herod executed James and threw Peter in prison. The Church prayed for Peter. At first there seemed no answer. But the night before Peter's trial, an angel rescued him from the high-security wing of the jail and led him to safety in the street outside. Peter made for what he knew was a safe house. Though it was the middle of the night people were there praying. They didn't have much confidence in their prayers being answered, because they couldn't believe he was at the door. 'Peter? It can't be Peter; Peter is in jail.' But he knocked so loud and so long they eventually took a look. It *was* Peter! God had answered their prayers.

What emerges from Acts is that the early Church was a praying Church. Prayer was not something to be fitted in between all the other activities, nor something for just the faithful few. Prayer together was top priority, perhaps the key to all the remarkable miracles the first Christians experienced. These people really valued prayer.

Today's prayer meetings

Given this impressive prioritising of communal prayer in the early Church, you'd think today's prayer meetings would be packed out. They're not. Today's average Christian does not go to a prayer meeting. Even those who campaign for more do not necessarily plan to attend them.

The reasons aren't hard to identify; it's just that no one normally admits them. Located in a cold, spartan church hall, seated on ancient and uncomfortable chairs, a dozen dedicated people sit with heads bowed. The list of prayer topics is read out. It's so long and detailed no one would remember it except it hasn't changed much from last week. Mrs McSherry still has arthritis; Mr Underwood doesn't have a date yet for his operation; Mr Williams remains in his bed of sickness; the pastor is in constant need of fresh inspiration; the missionaries need ever more encouragement in their difficult work; and so on, and on, and on. Thus it was last week, this week, and perhaps will be for evermore.

After years of meeting like this, it's hard to find new things to say, which is one reason why there are long silences between prayers. No one minds the silences, so they claim, for they're sure that everybody is deep in private prayer at those moments. Well, perhaps not Mrs Milne whose snoring becomes awkwardly audible, but the others are used to it now. The faithful pray on, never stopping until the clock reaches 9 p.m., at which precise moment there's a weekly miracle as everyone gets simultaneous guidance that it's time to finish. They rise from their seats, stretch their weary bones, and quietly acknowledge how important it's been they've met for prayer. Why, they wonder, don't others join them?

The answer is that today's generation has little appetite or stamina for a week after week experience which scales high peaks of dullness, often seems to achieve little, and can leave those who attend more spiritually depressed than uplifted. It requires a well-developed martyr instinct to survive. Most prayer meetings have to be endured; rarely can they be enjoyed. Therefore few attend and the majority feel guilty but glad that they don't.

Together for prayer?

'But prayer is important. We must pray.' Yes, we must, and that's biblical. So, is today's Church failing by not getting together more to pray? Probably not, for what's not biblical and highly questionable is any obligation to attend regular prayer meetings.

Often the Scripture passages quoted to prove the importance of prayer meetings are either vague or simply general references to prayer. Acts 2:42 is like that. Being told that the early Christians devoted themselves to prayer means only that they took prayer seriously, not necessarily that they were constantly in prayer huddles. They may have prayed entirely privately, or together but each saying their own prayers. As we'll see later with Jesus, Jews at prayer in those times were often individualistic, not communal in our usual sense. For example, Josephus, the Jewish writer of the first century, was at prayer in the synagogue at Tiberias when someone engaged him in conversation. Did that bring a prayer meeting to a halt? No. Only Josephus had his prayers interrupted. E.P. Sanders comments, 'People were in the synagogue, and it was time for prayer, but they were not all doing the same thing at the same instant' (E.P. Sanders, *Judaism: Practice and Belief* [SCM Press, 1992], pp.207–8). So caution is necessary. Just because there's a reference to prayer doesn't mean people were running a prayer meeting like we know today. Being devoted to prayer may mean something very different to what today's prayer meeting advocates have assumed.

Many other references to prayer are equally general: 'If you believe, you will receive whatever you ask for in prayer' (Matt. 21:22); 'Therefore I tell you, whatever you ask for in prayer, believe that you have received it, and it will be yours' (Mark 11:24); 'And I will do whatever you ask in my name, so that the Son may bring glory to the Father. You may ask me for anything in my name, and I will do it' (John 14:13–14).

There is every justification in using passages like these to urge the importance of prayer. There is no justification in using them to promote attendance at prayer meetings.

The same is true about prayer references in the New Testament letters. James has instructions for anyone who is sick. 'He should call the elders of the church to pray over him and anoint him with oil in the name of the Lord' (Jas. 5:14). That's a prayer gathering, but under very special and specific circumstances, and nothing like and no warrant for our general prayer meetings.

Paul encourages the Ephesians to 'pray in the Spirit on all occasions with all kinds of prayers and requests' (Eph. 6:18), tells the Romans to be 'joyful in hope, patient in affliction, faithful in prayer' (Rom. 12:12), and the Colossians to 'Devote yourselves to prayer, being watchful and thankful' (Col. 4:2).

These are powerful exhortations to prayer, but phrases

like 'all occasions' must mean more than 7.30 on a Wednesday evening.

Sometimes prayer is unmentioned when we'd have expected it to be to the fore. In 1 Corinthians 14 Paul lists several things the Christians did when they met with each other: 'When you come together, everyone has a hymn, or a word of instruction, a revelation, a tongue or an interpretation' (1 Cor. 14:26). Where's prayer? Ordinary everyday prayer isn't in the list. Throughout that chapter, in fact, prophecy and not prayer is singled out as the special activity.

Through all the New Testament letters, there's no reference to any meeting whose focus was solely prayer.

Prayer in Acts

Because Acts describes the key features of early Church life, we'd expect it to be littered with accounts of the Christians getting together to pray. It isn't. In fact there is not a single instance of a routine, regular prayer meeting.

Certainly they prayed while they waited for the Holy Spirit's power, though they did other things as well including the appointment of a new apostle. What happened in Acts 4 was not a prayer meeting. It was the reunion of Peter and John with the other Christians after being in jail and on trial, and the reunion culminated in one united prayer.

Surely there was a prayer meeting going on in Mary's home at the time of Peter's miraculous release from prison? Yes, there was but it was neither routine nor attended by everyone. It's hard to be sure how many believers were in Jerusalem at this time since persecution had forced many to leave. But it's likely there were still thousands. Mary's house may have been large, but not large enough for thousands! The vast majority weren't there. Especially significant is who in particular was absent. Peter says, 'Tell James and the brothers about this' (Acts 12:17). He's referring to his fellow church leaders in Jerusalem. They needed to know immediately that he'd escaped, so he wanted a message taken to them. But that means they weren't at the prayer meeting. It was a crucial time of prayer for the release of a key leader, and the top figures in the Church weren't there. Maybe this was just one of many crisis prayer meetings going on in Jerusalem. Hopefully Peter's fellow leaders were at another one. But if they were crisis meetings, they weren't routine. Peter was in jail and about to go on trial the next day. That's why they prayed. Acts 12 is wonderful evidence of two things: first, that some believers cared enough for Peter to sacrifice their sleep to pray for him, and second, that they believed that prayer worked (despite their incredulity when he appeared at the door). But that's all it is. Acts 12 is neither a whole church prayer meeting nor a regular event.

And there are no other references in Acts which could be used to argue for day by day or week by week communal prayer. There were times when specific groups prayed together for particular reasons, such as when Paul was leaving the Ephesian elders for what they all knew to be the final time (20:36). Even then it says only that Paul prayed.

That's as far as the record of Acts goes. What's shown is that when faced with crucial decisions, or anticipating huge events, or confronted by significant problems, they prayed together. That's all we know. If they met more often, more routinely, the Bible doesn't tell us.

Jesus and the disciples at prayer

We would expect the gospels to have many stories of Jesus and his disciples praying together, communal prayer which was substantial and meaningful, something with depth and power. They travelled together, slept together, worked together, faced opposition together. Surely they would also pray together (other than the Jewish equivalent of grace before meals). Jesus was teaching them about the

kingdom of God, demonstrating its power, and preparing
them to carry on his work when he left them. He must have
established a pattern of regular prayer with them, one which
the Church would follow later.

It's simply not there.

The most startling omission from all four gospels is any
account of Jesus praying with his disciples. It's worse than
that – there's evidence that Jesus took steps to avoid praying
with them. He chose to pray on his own. 'Very early in
the morning, while it was still dark, Jesus got up, left the
house and went off to a solitary place, where he prayed'
(Mark 1:35). Being alone for prayer wasn't unusual for
him. 'Jesus often withdrew to lonely places and prayed,'
Luke says (5:16). His isolation is reported again just before
he chose his apostles. 'One of those days Jesus went out
to a mountainside to pray, and spent the night praying to
God. When morning came, he called his disciples to him
. . .' (Luke 6:12–13). Another instance came when he left
the crowds he had fed miraculously. 'After he had dismissed
them, he went up on a mountainside by himself to pray.
When evening came, he was there alone' (Matt. 14:23).

Sometimes Jesus prayed on his own even when the disciples were nearby, for example just before Peter's famous
confession of him as 'Christ' at Caesarea Philippi. 'Once
when Jesus was praying in private and his disciples were
with him, he asked them, "Who do the crowds say I am?"'
(Luke 9:18). In other words, he was with the disciples,
but alone in his prayers. Much the same happened at the
Transfiguration. Jesus went up a mountain to pray, taking
Peter, John and James with him, yet there is a record only
of Jesus praying (Luke 9:29) and more than a hint that the
others were asleep (v. 32).

The supreme example of Jesus choosing to pray alone is
in Gethsemane, immediately prior to his arrest. Jesus was in
great distress – 'sorrowful', 'troubled', 'soul overwhelmed
to the point of death' are Matthew's descriptions (26:37–8).
More than any other time, Jesus seemed to need company.

Yet what did he tell his disciples? 'Sit here while I go over there and pray' (Matt. 26:36). He took the inner three of Peter, John and James to 'keep watch' with him (Matt. 26:38), but he didn't want them to pray beside him. Matthew says he went 'a little farther' (26:39) and Luke says it was 'a stone's throw beyond them' (22:41), and he prayed on his own. Back and forward he went to his disciples, rebuking them for not staying awake to pray, but never once kneeling alongside them. He wanted their support, but not to pray with them.

The nearest we ever get to Jesus praying with his disciples is when they ask him to teach them to pray. The context of that request is yet another occasion when Jesus prayed alone. Seeing his communication with God, the disciples realised the poverty of their prayer lives. 'One day Jesus was praying in a certain place. When he finished, one of his disciples said to him, "Lord, teach us to pray, just as John taught his disciples"' (Luke 11:1). So he did, and the result is what we call the Lord's Prayer (11:2–4). He taught them a prayer, or a model for prayer. The plural language (Give *us* each day . . .; Forgive *us our* sins . . .) shows it was a prayer someone could say on behalf of a group. It's unlikely that Jesus intended it to be recited in unison, and there's no evidence that the apostles used it that way.*

Jesus and his disciples simply did not pray together. They established no pattern for prayer meetings. In fact, their example is strong evidence against prayer meetings having any great significance in the plans of Jesus for his Church.

* If it was a prayer to be said together, it was unusual. 'In fact, first-century Jews probably did not do anything in unison . . . If Jews were in a synagogue at a time for prayer (e.g. first thing in the morning or at the time of the evening sacrifice in the temple), they may all have prayed, but not necessarily precisely the same prayer, and probably not in unison' (Sanders, p.207).

A special presence with the two or three?

What, then, of that apparently powerful argument that Jesus is specially present with his people when even two or three of them come together in his name?

He's not. The Matthew 18:20 reference is no justification for prayer meetings. Those who give the verse even a moment's examination will notice that prayer is never mentioned. 'For where two or three come together in my name, there am I with them,' is all Jesus said. Countless generations have chosen to take his words as a reference to communal prayer, but that's an assumption.

When a biblical verse has no explicit meaning, its sense must be understood from its context. The context of this verse nowhere mentions prayer. Instead it concerns disputes between Christians, how to resolve them, and how discipline is to be exercised when they can't be resolved. Here are the verses immediately before and after our key verse.

[15]'If your brother sins against you, go and show him his fault, just between the two of you. If he listens to you, you have won your brother over. [16]But if he will not listen, take one or two others along, so that "every matter may be established by the testimony of two or three witnesses." [17]If he refuses to listen to them, tell it to the church; and if he refuses to listen even to the church, treat him as you would a pagan or a tax collector.

[18]'I tell you the truth, whatever you bind on earth will be bound in heaven, and whatever you loose on earth will be loosed in heaven.

[19]'Again, I tell you that if two of you on earth agree about anything you ask for, it will be done for you by my Father in heaven. [20]For where two or three come together in my name, there am I with them.'

[21]Then Peter came to Jesus and asked, 'Lord, how many times shall I forgive my brother when he sins against me? Up to seven times?'

²²Jesus answered, 'I tell you, not seven times, but seventy-seven times.'

To understand verse 20, verses 18 and 19 are crucial. Jesus gives power to the Church to exercise disciplinary authority over its members, and seems to say decisions made on earth will be accepted in heaven. How could that be? Because when they meet in his name to make those decisions, Jesus himself is with them. Where two or three come together to represent his authority, they have his presence.

Paul told the Corinthians something similar when they needed to apply discipline in a case of extreme moral lapse.

Even though I am not physically present, I am with you in spirit. And I have already passed judgment on the one who did this, just as if I were present. When you are assembled in the name of our Lord Jesus and I am with you in spirit, and the power of our Lord Jesus is present, hand this man over to Satan, so that the sinful nature may be destroyed and his spirit saved on the day of the Lord. (1 Cor. 5:3–5)

There is, of course, a spiritual difference between Paul being with the Corinthians and Jesus being with his disciples when discipline is exercised, but the idea is like that in Matthew 18:20.

Therefore, when Jesus said that 'where two or three come together in my name, there am I with them' he was talking about his presence when judgments were being made. He was not teaching a greater spiritual or physical nearness to his disciples when they came together for prayer, as if you walked to the prayer meeting without Christ but encountered him when the first prayer was offered. Jesus really is with his people *all* the time, and is not *more* with his people when they gather for prayer. Jesus wasn't even saying that we become subjectively more aware of his presence, as if concentrating our minds in prayer helps us sense him in the midst. Matthew 18:20 isn't talking about prayer. It's talking about authority to back judgments. Therefore it's no basis for prayer meetings.

The good and the bad of prayer meetings

Prayer meetings can be good things. I have led many, and attended countless more. Some (not many, I confess) have been among those special experiences when a whole group felt caught up to heaven. God seemed so near, and his presence in the room was almost tangible. Those were wonderful times.

Prayer meetings also have several distinct advantages over solitary prayer: a) an imposed discipline – meetings happen at particular times, and you need to organise your life to be there; b) a stimulus to pray for things it would never occur to you to pray about if you were on your own; c) a rhythm of concerned prayer beating heavenward week by week, often bringing the deepest needs of a church over and over to the Father; d) companionship and encouragement that spurs everyone to pray more, and carries them through hard times when persevering in prayer is difficult.

Prayer with fellow Christians who share your concerns and share your passion to seek God can be an uplifting and powerful experience. People like me who engage in Christian ministry should realise that so much of the fruit we see from our work is in answer to the faithful prayers of those who gather and pour out their hearts to God for us. The prayers of God's people really matter.

But prayer meetings also have a downside. They carry three particular dangers.

One is that they can become a comfortable alternative to doing Christian work. If church life is riddled with 'form a committee' mentality when there are tasks to be done, then there's equally a 'let's pray about it' mentality. Prayer should lead to action, but easily becomes an alternative to action. The world will not be saved by prayer, and we must not pander to a form of pietism that wants to retreat into more and more prayer times when it's time to get on with God's work.

The second danger is the negative image of prayer which many prayer meetings give to young and not so young converts. My earlier description of a typical prayer meeting is not much exaggerated for still too many churches. It's hard to imagine a more dreary and dishonouring way of talking to the creator and Father of the universe. We have made communion with the Almighty crushingly mundane and – despite our fine words – apparently irrelevant. Praying together ought to offer a different and perhaps more inspiring dynamic compared to praying alone. Usually it's a worse dynamic. We don't need novelty, but we do need creativity. At present a high percentage of prayer meetings do more damage than good to the cause of prayer in Christ's Church.

The third danger is to those who don't attend regular prayer meetings. When we're told that the spiritual health of the church depends on the number attending the prayer meeting, those who don't come are subtly or unsubtly made to feel responsible for the church's problems. That would be fair if the Bible taught that corporate prayer is the critical factor for a church's life and ministry. But it doesn't. No one should be made to feel guilty for breaking what is not God's law. It's time for that burden to be lifted from those who don't attend the routine prayer meeting.

The New Testament teaches that prayer is important – there's no dispute about that – and shows people praying together when there was special reason why they should. But that's as far as the New Testament goes. It neither prescribes regular prayer meetings nor teaches that churches which don't have them, or have only a few attending, are spiritually sick.

That should be good news for many. It is for me, especially since I've also discovered a photographic society which meets on a *Thursday*. I wonder if they have any membership vacancies?

13

I'm saved because I made a decision

The warm glow deep inside grew steadily stronger. The mission team was telling of dramatic conversions and I was loving it. They'd crossed the Atlantic at their own expense so they could help our church with evangelism. Now, at the end of our week of mission, we'd joined with other teams for a 'victory banquet'. Each mission leader was taking turns to report. Frank, who had brought the team to our church, was talking in Technicolor splendour. 'On door-to-door visitation we met Mary. We asked the two Evangelism Explosion questions, gave her the rest of the presentation, and she received Christ right there and then. And the kids at the high school. We ran a club for them after classes each day. First day they poured in, bright faced and eager to learn. We gave them all New Testaments and they were back the next afternoon with their friends. Before we'd finished the week, a dozen of them had given their lives to Christ.'

On Frank went, detailing other conversions: the next-door neighbour of one of the church members; someone else's mother; a business colleague; three or four guests who had come to the Sunday service. And then there was Ben.

'Ben is Joanne's husband. She was never sure what he believed or what he wanted from life. We put the gospel to him straight. That made him think. He held off right until the last night of our mission. Then he came to me and said he needed Christ. We got down on our knees right where we were, not caring that everyone was looking, and he asked Jesus into his life. Now he's a changed man. And there are many more. Let me tell you there are now another fifty Christians at the church because of the mission.'

Frank wasn't telling lies. All his stories were true, including the one about Ben because I'd seen them get down on their knees. Some great things had happened. And apparently our experience wasn't unique. Virtually every mission team had similar accounts to bring. One even described how a whole school had received Christ. We'd had a taste of revival.

Next Sunday I was at church early, checking there were enough seats out to cope with the extra numbers. How good it would be to welcome so many brand new Christians.

They didn't come. Only one or two of those who had been contacted during the mission turned up, and those were people we already knew well. None of the kids from school were there, and no one from door-to-door visitation. The high expectations crashlanded; the special sermon targeting the new Christians was wasted. My disappointment only increased over the next few weeks. Hardly any of those who'd made professions of faith lasted. That included Ben. Part of him tried to change, but really he wanted the benefits of the gospel without any cost to his lifestyle. He came, fell away, came back all repentant, then fell away again all too quickly. Eventually he stopped coming back. Later I heard that 'the whole school came to Christ' report was little more than a hands-up response at the end of a school assembly. The local church didn't have to find new premises to cope with the attendance at services.

With hindsight, my charitable perspective on those events was that those who came on mission wanted to believe these fifty people around our church had all been converted. It meant their trip wasn't wasted, and gave them something worthwhile to report back home. My less charitable perspective was that a wholly inappropriate doctrine of conversion was at work, one which equates salvation with a 'walk to the front, bow your head and pledge your life' experience.

It seems these people were making acts of commitment but not being soundly converted. They had been told they could be instantly saved simply by receiving Christ there and then. Was that wrong?

Is instant conversion biblical?

Evangelistic preachers – including me – don't hesitate to offer immediate salvation. 'Tonight your whole direction for eternity can be changed. There's no waiting period and no apprenticeship. You don't have to make yourself good enough for God. You can't anyway. Give your life to Jesus and God will accept you just as you are. You came in guilty and separated from God. You can leave this building forgiven and a child of God. You can be born again now. All you have to do is give your life to Christ.' I've said words like those, and I've seen people respond. Sometimes they walk to the front at the end of the service, sometimes they pray quietly where they are. Sometimes they simply make their decision, and no one knows until later.

Biblically there's nothing wrong here. John 3:16 says, 'For God so loved the world that he gave his one and only Son, that whoever believes in him shall not perish but have eternal life.' Verses like that don't describe salvation by stages: start disbelieving in God and disliked by him; move in time to showing interest and thus becoming more acceptable; eventually reach full commitment and be saved. Such a process would make eternal life a distant goal, whereas the gospel portrays it as something to be grasped there and then. People hear the gospel, truly believe, and from that precise moment have their destiny changed. They often have little understanding about Christ, but with simple faith they reach out to him. In grace he hears their stumbling words of commitment, and gives them a new life.

A good example is Zacchaeus, the wealthy tax collector whom Christ called out of his tree perch in order to have a meal with him. We don't know the conversation which took place over that meal, but we do know its outcome: Zacchaeus started giving his money away, partly to the poor and partly to repay anyone he'd cheated. Jesus, seeing the change, pronounced: 'Today salvation has come to this house, because this man, too, is a son of Abraham. For the Son of Man came to seek and to save what was lost' (Luke 19:9–10). At that moment, the moment Zacchaeus showed he wanted a new life, Jesus declared him to be saved.

There was also immediate salvation for one of the two thieves crucified alongside Jesus. Unlike his companion, this man refused to ridicule Jesus, and said, ' "Jesus, remember me when you come into your kingdom." Jesus answered him, "I tell you the truth, today you will be with me in paradise" ' (Luke 23:42–3). Nothing could be simpler. The dying robber made a rudimentary confession of faith, and Jesus assured him he'd be in heaven that very day.

The conversion of Saul who became Paul, the great apostle, was equally sudden. On his way to imprison Christians in Damascus he was struck to the ground, and heard the voice of Christ. Later he was visited in Damascus by Ananias who told him, 'And now what are you waiting for? Get up, be baptised and wash your sins away, calling on his name' (Acts 22:16). That was it. Saul was converted. He arrived wanting to put Christians to death; within days he was preaching alongside them.

In one of his letters Paul made the definitive statement about the sudden switch conversion brings. 'Therefore, if anyone is in Christ, he is a new creation; the old has gone, the new has come!' (2 Cor. 5:17). There, in a nutshell, is the instantaneously transformed life. It's like the change of status a wedding brings. Before my wedding service I was single; from the moment the service was over I was married. The old had gone, the new had come. So it is in respect of the relationship with God for the person who has become a Christian.

Without question the Bible teaches immediate conversion.

Of course it doesn't have to be that way. Some become Christians gradually. They grow into faith, and can't identify one special moment when they first trusted Christ. They're like someone on a long-haul flight who falls asleep, and wakens only at touchdown in a far-off city. As he steps off the plane, he looks around and all is different. He doesn't know when he arrived in the new land, he just knows he has. A spiritual journey like that is as authentic as a dramatic and instantaneous conversion experience. What matters is reaching the 'new land' of God's kingdom, not how someone gets there.

So, there's validity for both the slow and fast routes into the kingdom. But, as a pastor, I was finding all too many of those in the sudden change category backed off after a while. I knew people of all sorts of experience could fall away – the parable of the sower has three out of four types of seed failing to bear fruit – but there seemed to be a particular problem with those who had had sudden conversion experiences.

Three clues

I got my first clue to what was wrong when I visited the fifty people who professed to have become Christians during the week of mission in my church. Virtually all really believed they were saved. They had been told that if they bowed their heads and asked Jesus to forgive their sins, then they would have eternal life.

Those who told them that – the visiting mission team – also believed those they left behind were now Christians. As far as the missioners were concerned, these people had given their lives to Jesus. Whatever followed, whether or not they came to church and lived as Christians should, they'd made a decision for Christ, and therefore they were converted. Famous hymn words had been fulfilled:

> *'Tis done, the great transaction's done!*
> *I am my Lord's, and He is mine!*

A second clue emerged when I realised this wasn't the first time I'd been given confident reassurances about the salvation of people who were now far away from any real Christian faith. Those reassurances had come from parents who had remained firmly convinced about the conversions of their children, even though they'd turned their backs on anything to do with Christianity as they moved through the teen years and into adulthood. 'When he was seven,' one mother told me, 'he prayed a prayer asking Jesus into his heart. So I know he'll be saved.' The son she was talking about, now aged twenty, had a lifestyle written on one of hell's prescription pads. But, I was assured, there had been a moment in his life when he'd accepted Christ, so he was all right.

My third clue came when I remembered what my father had told me about the church to which he'd belonged when he was younger. It had a huge congregation of nearly two thousand members. You'd think they'd have needed a vast sanctuary or multiple services to get all these people in. They didn't. Most never came, and the church building rarely reached its modest capacity of 400. The only time it was packed was on special communion Sundays. Communion had to be attended periodically to retain membership, so the minister put on extra services to cope with the crowds. About fifteen hundred of those who came for communion were never seen the rest of the time.

I realised there are still many churches like that. Their membership lists have a high percentage of people who are nominal in their belief. Some are nominal because they inherited an empty form of Christianity from their parents, but others are nominal who showed initial enthusiasm but then drifted away. They never overtly rejected Christianity, but now they don't think much about it. They don't attend church nor do they worry about trying to live to please Christ. Ask them if they consider themselves Christians, and they'll be offended that you asked. Of course they are, and they'll often tell you the date and event when they were saved.

Life membership of the Christian club

When I put my three clues together I saw that what they had in common was one particular idea of what becoming a Christian was all about. These people looked to the 'experience', the 'encounter', the 'prayer of commitment', like someone else would to the moment they took out life membership of a club.

I have a life membership of the Student Association of the university at which I studied. I'd like to say that it's a great honour to have been granted it. I'd like to say that, but it wouldn't be true. All I had to do to get life membership was belong to the Association while I was a student and pay a fee after I graduated. The privileges of the Association are a low-cost restaurant and discounted beer. One of those seemed of value to me, so I handed over my money. Now there's nothing further I have to do or pay to remain a member. I can take advantage of my membership as much or as little as I want. If I never use the facilities or if I go there every day, both are equally okay, for my one-off payment conferred all the benefits of membership on me permanently, and what I do with them is up to me.

Many think they join Christianity just like that. What do you have to do to get eternal life? You need to have an experience of Christ. How do you get that? You walk to the front after an evangelistic appeal, or ask God to take away your sins, or invite Christ to be your Saviour. The experience may be dramatic and emotional or it may be serene and thoughtful. As long as it happens.

Now, response made, you've met all the conditions there are for life membership of the Christian club. The preacher or counsellor told you that if you came to Christ you'd have eternal life. You wouldn't be on a course of probation for it; you wouldn't be paying it up by monthly instalments. You'd actually have it for ever from that moment on. So you did as you were told, and now eternal life is yours.

Paying the insurance premium

Some don't look on their 'encounter' like taking out life membership of a club. They have another image in mind: insurance.

Insurance has been around for a long time. For ordinary mortals, it used to come in only a few varieties: your life, your home and its contents, and your car if you had one. These days we insure almost anything. I'm urged to arrange insurance for my health, for my mortgage and for my holiday plans. If I take out a loan I'm advised to get insurance in case I can't pay it off. A brochure for accident insurance priced all the disabilities I might suffer. Honestly, I'd never realised how valuable some parts of my body are. One scheme will protect me from claims arising out of my photography (is it that bad?), while another promises to compensate those I maim while playing golf (it *is* that bad). I could insure against pet bills if my dog was not already so old as to be uninsurable. My wife and I are at the age where no one bothers now to offer us insurance against pregnancy, though the older you get the more you might value it.

So, our modern society is thoroughly familiar with the concept of insurance. To avoid or minimise difficulties or disasters in the future, we pay premiums up front. Then, if anything goes wrong, we're protected. Insurance buys us peace of mind.

Exactly that mentality is brought to Christian commitment by many. They've been told that they're sinners, and the price for sin is death – eternal death. Once they feel the heat of hellfire, it'll be too late to put anything right. What can they do to escape such a dreadful end? Answer: buy fire insurance while there's still time. An encounter with

Christ is the premium. Just as a small cash investment up front can yield a big financial return long-term in ordinary insurance, so a small investment in religion will provide a big spiritual return in the longest of terms, eternity. They'll cover themselves against judgment and hell by a premium paid to Christ now. That premium is a public commitment, and maybe they'll supplement it with occasional top-up payments of appearances at church. The package should protect them for ever.

After that there's nothing else that needs to be done. As with all insurance, once you've paid your premium you can sit back in quiet comfort or even get a little reckless. You'll be all right no matter what happens. Those who have brought an insurance mentality to their Christian commitment behave exactly like that. Some relax spiritually, trusting that what they've done is enough for salvation. Some live foolish lives, but are confident they'll be saved. They've paid their premium by their one-off pledge to Christ.

A wedding but no marriage

Those who have never followed up their 'experience' of Christ are usually afflicted by one of these two ways of thinking, the club membership or the insurance premium. Both forms are seriously flawed in respect of Christianity.

Imagine a wedding without a marriage. The couple make great plans for their special day. There's so much to do in advance: a church and minister to book for the service; a hotel or restaurant for the reception (the real main event); dresses and suits to be bought; flowers to be arranged; photographer to be chosen; invitations to be sent out; cars to be hired; speeches to be prepared. And a hundred more things to be done. The big day comes. It's non-stop. The early appointment with the hairdresser, hours of putting on make-up, being overwhelmed during the vows, posing for more photos afterwards than in the whole of life preceding, eating, drinking and dancing at the reception, trying to speak to every single person who has come. It's a whirl of activity. But it's great. It's exhilarating. It has cost a king's ransom, but, for that special and unique day, it's been worth it.

It's also been exhausting. So, as the evening wears on, the groom and bride meet in a quiet corner. 'Thank you for making the day so special,' he whispers tenderly. 'Thank *you*,' she says, 'I've loved every minute of it.' Then, with a gentle kiss, they part. He goes back to his flat; she goes home to be with her parents. It was a wonderful day. Everyone thought so. But it's over now. There never was going to be anything else.

Sadly, tragically, and dangerously, that's what many 'experiences' of Christ amount to. They're splendid and wonderful, but they lead on to nothing. They ought to have been the beginning of a beautiful and lasting relationship, but they become ends in themselves. There's no marriage there. They are unconsummated encounters. That's not how it was meant to be.

The call was to be a disciple

Jesus invited no one to a one-off experience. He called people to a life of discipleship.

Among the first to be changed by Jesus's preaching were men like Simon, Andrew, James, John and Matthew. The first four of these were all fishermen. Jesus called them while they were working. ' "Come, follow me," Jesus said, "and I will make you fishers of men." At once they left their nets and followed him' (Matt. 4:19–20). That response from Simon and Andrew was apparently without hesitation. It was no less from James and John, even though they had the added complication of a working partnership with their father. 'Jesus called them, and immediately they left the boat and their father and followed him' (Matt. 4:21–2).

As well as the promptness of their decisions, there are

two significant details. One, Jesus called them to a task. He didn't merely meet with them, talk with them and give them new insights. They were to follow him and become new kinds of fishermen, fishing for men for God's kingdom. Two, Jesus required them to leave their present lifestyles. To follow Jesus they had to give up their work and their families. They didn't merely fit Jesus in to how they were living; he revolutionised how they were living.

It was very similar with Matthew. 'As Jesus went on from there, he saw a man named Matthew sitting at the tax collector's booth. "Follow me," he told him, and Matthew got up and followed him' (Matt. 9:9). After two thousand years and so much familiarity with the story, we can't easily appreciate the immensity of the decision Matthew made, and what a change this was in his life. While the others could probably return to fishing if the venture with Jesus didn't work out, Matthew would never be able to go back to tax collecting. When he walked away from his booth, he walked away from wealth and security. Meeting Jesus was not a fleeting, transitory experience, nor some quick investment in his spiritual future. This encounter had consequences which affected every day of his life from then on.

And, as soon as we look closely, we see that's how it was for others. Their conversions may have been instantaneous, but the effects of their conversions were long-term. Zacchaeus made a public pronouncement of a new life, one no one would allow him to forget. Paul's conversion was in semi-privacy, but quickly became very public. He had not been saved merely for his own well-being; he had been saved for a task. 'You will be his witness to all men of what you have seen and heard' (Acts 22:15). And he got on with the work immediately. 'At once he began to preach in the synagogues that Jesus is the Son of God. All those who heard him were astonished . . .' (Acts 9:20–1). Of course they were astonished. He'd come to destroy Christians, and now he was one. Paul's conversion must have quickly become one of the hottest pieces of gossip and scandal in

Damascus and then Jerusalem. It would be obvious to all that he was a changed man. Many that Christ met were changed: Bartimaeus got his sight and then followed Jesus; a Gadarene man was set free from demons and wanted to go with Jesus, but instead was sent home to tell people how much God had done for him; Mary Magdalene was freed from seven demons and perhaps an immoral lifestyle and became one of a small group of women who journeyed with Jesus and the Twelve; a Samaritan woman met at a well, whose life was an open book to Jesus, became his P.R. agent to the rest of the Samaritans. Even the thief dying on a cross alongside Jesus had a new future – not much of it in this world, but for ever with Christ in paradise. The call of Jesus was never to a one-off experience, but always to a new life. He invited people to discipleship, to a lasting and life-changing relationship, to a 'marriage' and not merely a 'wedding'.

Those who accepted were commanded to give the same invitation to others. 'Therefore go and make disciples of all nations, baptising them in the name of the Father and of the Son and of the Holy Spirit, and teaching them to obey everything I have commanded you. And surely I am with you always, to the very end of the age' (Matt. 28:19–20).

This Great Commission was to make those who didn't know Jesus into his disciples. That would require them to make a total surrender of their lives to God, and to learn everything Jesus had taught the first believers. In other words, they were to become the same kind of disciples as Matthew, James, John, Andrew, Peter and the rest. And, just as he had been with them, he would always be with these new disciples too. The change in people's lives would be enormous. The blessings which would follow that change would also be enormous.

It would never be enough for anyone to have a here today, gone tomorrow encounter with Christ's goodness; Christians were to have a whole new life.

Because the apostles understood that, they nurtured the

first converts when they came along. With three thousand after the Day of Pentecost, it was quite a task. But their new life – new discipline – began immediately. 'They devoted themselves to the apostles' teaching and to the fellowship, to the breaking of bread and to prayer. All the believers were together and had everything in common. Every day they continued to meet together in the temple courts. They broke bread in their homes and ate together with glad and sincere hearts' (Acts 2:42, 44, 46).

These people had new loyalties, new priorities and new practices. The Day of Pentecost experience was not an end in itself. It was the beginning of a radically different way of living.

Missing, presumed lost

In sharp contrast are those who stuck with the faith for a short time, but then backed off. The New Testament has nothing good to say about them.

Jesus is the first to use hard words, describing unfruitful seed being snatched away by Satan, or scared away by trouble or persecution, or lured away by the concerns and attractions of this world (Mark 4:13–19). In at least the last two of these cases, the seed had begun to take root. A plant came into being. But it never grew to become the fruitful crop it was meant to be, and it was lost.

Jesus is even more blunt with other images. The last servant in the parable of the talents is entrusted with just one talent. He buries it so he'll be able to return it one day to his master. He neither loses it nor steals it. He simply fails to do anything positive with it. For that he pays the highest price, as his master commands, 'Throw that worthless servant outside, into the darkness, where there will be weeping and gnashing of teeth' (Matt. 25:30).

The much-loved analogy of Jesus as the vine and his Father as the gardener contains terrifying words. 'He cuts off every branch in me that bears no fruit . . . If anyone

does not remain in me, he is like a branch that is thrown
away and withers; such branches are picked up, thrown
into the fire and burned' (John 15:2, 6). Obviously Jesus
is not referring to people with no knowledge of him. Nor
can he be speaking about those who have heard but never
responded, for he's describing 'every branch *in me* that bears
no fruit'. So, those who are discarded and burned are people
with some real experience of being in him but who do not
go on to bear fruit. They are not merely pruned, like the
fruit bearing branches ('. . . every branch that does bear
fruit he prunes so that it will be even more fruitful' [John
15:2]). Rather, with brutal imagery, Jesus says the unfruitful
branches are cut off and thrown away. If they thought they
had life membership, they were wrong. If they imagined they
had fully comprehensive insurance against all eventualities,
they were deceived.

Jesus took a hard line. Later on, the early Church
was no softer on converts who didn't live up to their
commitment.

Leading the blacklist were Ananias and Sapphira. When
many were liquidising their property assets so the proceeds
were available for communal use, this couple also sold up.
However, Ananias didn't hand over all he got for the sale.
'With his wife's full knowledge he kept back part of the
money for himself, but brought the rest and put it at the
apostles' feet' (Acts 5:2). Now, we wouldn't reckon this
much of a sin. Did they need to give anything? No. Did
they in fact make a large offering? Yes. They chose to
sell their own home or land, and probably handed over
the largest portion to the church. We'd consider Ananias
and Sapphira very generous. They'd be valuable church
members. Their only sin was exaggeration. They pretended
they gave everything when actually they kept some back.
If every Christian who exaggerated today dropped dead,
the Church would be littered with corpses. We don't rank
such minor deceit as important. Peter did not consider this
minor deceit. 'Ananias, how is it that Satan has so filled

your heart that you have lied to the Holy Spirit and have kept for yourself some of the money you received for the land? What made you think of doing such a thing? You have not lied to men but to God' (Acts 5:3, 4). Ananias promptly fell down dead. When his wife was confronted similarly, she also died.

These people had experienced Christ, perhaps among the three thousand converted at Pentecost. They'd been baptised in water, received the power of the Holy Spirit, seen the apostles perform miracles, felt the building shake after prayer, and given over the greatest part of their property for the communal good. But none of that exempted them from the obligations of discipleship. They failed to live out their faith – they lied – and for that they fell under a judgment which was immediate and drastic.

There were others who also backed off from their initial commitment and so came under condemnation. Hymenaeus and Alexander rejected their faith and a good conscience and thus 'shipwrecked their faith' (1 Tim. 1:19–20). Phygelus and Hermogenes were Paul's companions until the going got tough, and then they got going – they walked out on him (2 Tim. 1:15). Demas did much the same, deserting Paul because 'he loved this world' (2 Tim. 4:10). As for Alexander (either the same or a different man to the one mentioned earlier – no one is sure), he is firmly denounced. 'Alexander the metalworker did me a great deal of harm. The Lord will repay him for what he has done' (2 Tim. 4:14). William Barclay thinks he may have been a renegade Christian who turned informer against Paul, making false allegations to cause Paul trouble (William Barclay, *The Letters to Timothy, Titus and Philemon* [The Saint Andrew Press, 1960], p. 252). Whatever his crime, Alexander's eternal prospects were poor. The outlook was bleak for all these people who had begun well but finished badly. They couldn't live today off what had been true for them yesterday.

In fact, Paul specifically warned his readers not to rely

on their past Christian experiences. He didn't. 'I beat my body and make it my slave so that after I have preached to others, I myself will not be disqualified for the prize' (1 Cor. 9:27). But the Corinthians seemed to think their eternal prize was already in the bag. Paul gave them an Old Testament illustration. The Israelites, in their exodus from slavery in Egypt, all experienced supernatural phenomena. 'Our forefathers were all under the cloud and ... all passed through the sea. They were all baptised into Moses in the cloud and in the sea. They all ate the same spiritual food and drank the same spiritual drink; for they drank from the spiritual rock that accompanied them, and that rock was Christ' (1 Cor. 10:1–4). Paul's way of using the Old Testament is difficult for us, but the point he's making is not. These Jewish forefathers were rescued by God, and had blessings equivalent to those now enjoyed by Christians. So, with all that behind them, were the Israelites safe from spiritual harm? No, they weren't. 'Nevertheless, God was not pleased with most of them; their bodies were scattered over the desert' (v.5). Such a downfall could happen again. 'Now these things occurred as examples to keep us from setting our hearts on evil things as they did' (v.6). In the Israelites' case the 'evil things' were idolatry and immorality, but they could have been anything. Thousands upon thousands of them died, up to twenty-three thousand in one day (v.8). Though they'd been saved from Egypt by God and supernaturally provided for, their failure to live rightly meant they were eventually lost. The Corinthians, trusting in their Christian experiences, had better take heed. 'These things happened to them as examples and were written down as warnings for us, on whom the fulfilment of the ages has come. So, if you think you are standing firm, be careful that you don't fall!' (vv.11–12).

It would be wonderful to excise these sentences from Scripture, but they're there. At the very least Paul's warning is: 'There are people who have pledged their lives to Christ and had many wonderful spiritual experiences, but they're not living now as disciples should, and therefore they'll be lost.' It won't do to have a one-off encounter with Christ – no matter how splendid or meaningful at the time – and then forget all about it.

So near, yet so far away

The idea that a one-time decision for Christ guarantees access to heaven and grants immunity from hell is not Christianity. It may be near Christianity but it's not Christianity.

A genuine encounter with Christ which leads to a long-term relationship between Lord and servant, that is the gospel. A brief flirtation with little or nothing beyond it of day by day discipleship, that is not the gospel.

I fear now for those fifty who were contacted during our church's mission. I wish they'd think again about Christ. But I suspect they won't. Patients who think they're cured don't seek healing. Without a sense of spiritual illness why should the fifty bother with a spiritual cure, especially one that is far more demanding than the convenient and comfortable 'get saved quick' gospel they've believed already? It gives them assurance, a false assurance which is about the worst thing they could have because it paralyses them spiritually. They're in desperate danger, and, if they don't see that soon, they'll be lost.

Some of the seven churches of Asia to which the living Christ dictated letters were in precisely that state. Jesus didn't pull his punches with them.

- To Ephesus: 'Yet I hold this against you: You have forsaken your first love. Remember the height from which you have fallen! Repent and do the things you did at first. If you do not repent, I will come to you and remove your lampstand from its place' (Rev. 2:4–5).
- To Sardis: 'These are the words of him who holds the

seven spirits of God and the seven stars. I know your deeds; you have a reputation of being alive, but you are dead. Wake up! Strengthen what remains and is about to die, for I have not found your deeds complete in the sight of my God. Remember, therefore, what you have received and heard; obey it, and repent. But if you do not wake up, I will come like a thief, and you will not know at what time I will come to you' (Rev. 3:1–3).

- To Laodicea: 'I know your deeds, that you are neither cold nor hot. I wish you were either one or the other! So, because you are lukewarm – neither hot nor cold – I am about to spit you out of my mouth' (Rev. 3:15–16).

Those warnings were blunt. They weren't heeded, and every one of the churches went out of existence.

On the whole we're not as honest with people as Christ is. We don't want to offend them by suggesting they're not Christians. How many are we allowing to go to hell unoffended?

I visited a church which had two thousand five hundred members, though less than half that number attended. Every week the church mailed its newsletter to all these people. If any member had a particular need of the church's ministry – perhaps they were in hospital, perhaps they were getting married, perhaps a family member had died – then it was taken for granted that the ministers would rush to provide what was wanted. People liked belonging to that church. Yet, privately, one of the pastors told me he was uncomfortable about having so many on the roll who were not living out their faith.

'Why do you allow it?' I asked innocently.

He looked sheepish. 'Some people like us to have a high membership. It reads well in the denominational return.' He paused, then brightened, 'And we always hope that by mailing out the newsletter, one week they'll think again about Christianity and do something about their commitment.'

'They'll think again about Christianity only if you *don't* mail them the newsletter and instead write to them saying you're taking their name off the membership roll,' I said.

The pastor looked at me, and quietly nodded.

As far as I know, nothing changed and many people there, and here, and everywhere go on thinking they're all right for heaven because once upon a time they 'made a decision' for Christ. Which, I wonder, will be the greater tragedy on judgment day: those who are lost because we never told them about Jesus, or those who are lost because we told them but allowed them to think that beginning the race was enough, and it didn't matter about finishing?

'See to it, brothers, that none of you has a sinful, unbelieving heart that turns away from the living God. We have come to share in Christ if we hold firmly till the end the confidence we had at first' (Heb. 3:12, 14).

14

God will allow nothing to come into my life greater than I can bear

John died and Margaret, his wife, was left alone. It ended a very special relationship, for Margaret had nursed John day and night since he'd been seriously hurt in an industrial accident twenty years earlier. After an early phase of adjustment, caring for John had seemed no burden to Margaret. Though he was often not well – he never worked again – they were able to go places and do things. Perhaps because he was disabled and needed Margaret's care, and perhaps because they had so much time for each other, they had a depth of love, a level of understanding and a quality of intimacy which were among the best any marriage could produce. They were supremely happy.

But relationships and life on this earth are not for ever. John grew weaker, Margaret cared for him as long as she could, but then he died.

Almost all of Margaret's world had been John. He'd filled every thought, every minute, and his needs had been the reason for every action. Margaret's life was suddenly purposeless. She sank into deep grief, a grief that never lifted as the months went past.

'They tell me that after a year I should have got over John's death,' she said one time I visited her. I reassured her that every bereavement is as unique as the relationship which has been lost, that no one else could know what she was feeling, and she shouldn't listen to people who put pressure on her.

But when I saw her next, the advice-givers had been busy again. 'They say that since I'm a Christian God will allow nothing to come into my life greater than I can bear.' Margaret looked at me steadily for a moment, and then her eyes filled and tears flowed. 'But I can't bear it! I can't bear losing John. I can't bear being alone.'

Margaret voiced what others fear to say. They know that, as Christians, God won't let them be pushed beyond their limits, yet beyond their limits and cracking under the strain is precisely where they find themselves.

Andrew was like that. He was a sincere Christian, trying hard to use his many gifts for God. He was the rising star of the company which employed him, a young executive with a real flair for management, inspiring loyalty and hard work from others. Jealous colleagues looked on and tried to analyse his technique. But they could never find it, for Andrew had no technique other than respecting people and treating them fairly. Because they felt valued, his staff gave their best for Andrew.

But, like many other middle managers in the corporate jungle, the reward Andrew got for success was ever more demanding goals. His workload was increased, and the next year increased again. For a time Andrew revelled in the challenge. Everyone pitched in, worked solidly through the day and often after hours as well. The goals were met. In fact, productivity was so good senior management told Andrew they were sure he could get by with fewer staff, and left him to choose who to dismiss. That really hurt Andrew. People had sacrificed for him and the firm, and to tell some of them that they no longer had a job felt to Andrew like betrayal. Even after that the pressure was turned up again: more output needed but less of a budget with which to achieve it.

Andrew's confidence, motivation and discipline began to break. He kept having to work late, and missed meals

with his young family. When he got home, he was so
exhausted that he couldn't drag himself along to the
church for meetings which at one time he'd relished.
Instead he slumped listlessly in a chair, staring without
seeing at a flickering TV screen. He felt he was failing in
his marriage, failing in his Christianity, and, as the targets
became increasingly impossible, failing in his work. 'I ought
to be able to cope,' was the nearest he ever got to admitting
that he wasn't.

Thankfully, there was no dramatic breakdown for
Andrew. All that happened was that he came home
from work one day and told his wife he'd handed in his
resignation. He was six months without a job, and then
found something far less demanding. After that he was a
happier man, though there were still the nagging questions,
'Surely I should have been able to keep going? Surely, with
God's help, I should have survived anything?'

Andrew's questions, and the advice given to Margaret,
make good sense. The logic is simple and compelling: 'I am
a child of God, loved by my heavenly Father. When I have
a need I can draw on his strength. Because his strength is
unlimited, I can therefore face any problem, any hardship,
any pressure he allows to come my way.'

Surviving with God's help

Sure enough, the Bible is full of people who faced enor-
mously difficult situations and came through because God
helped them.

Gideon was given the job of leading his broken, demoralised and frightened nation against invading Midianites.
It would have been a near impossible job for a supremely
skilled commander. For Gideon it was unthinkable. He
described himself as the weakest member of the weakest
clan (Judg. 6:15). All he wanted was to hide away in a
wine press to thresh his wheat. Never was there a more
unpromising leader. But God commissioned him anyway.

To make sure he trusted only in God, and that God alone got the glory for victory, Gideon was stripped of most of the army he'd raised. Eventually he attacked the massive forces of Midian with just 300 soldiers, but the rout was complete and Israel was released from oppression. The task had been immense but with God's power it was done (Judg. 7).

The same could be said with Elijah. He was the lone prophet of God on Mount Carmel, facing 450 prophets of Baal in a life or death contest. The test was to see whether the Lord or Baal would supernaturally light a sacrifice. The false prophets danced around their altar for hours, shouting loudly and slashing themselves in a frenzy of devotion and persuasion directed at their god. Of course, no one answered. Then it was Elijah's turn. He made the task doubly hard by having the altar he'd built drenched in water. Then he knelt to pray. Immediately God's fire fell and burnt up not only the sacrifice but the altar as well. It was a remarkable triumph. Nothing about it could have been done by Elijah in his own strength. God had come close to his servant and shown what he could do (1 Kings 18).

Daniel's experience was no less dramatic. Arrested for breaking a law which banned prayer, Daniel was sentenced to death by being thrown to the lions. As night fell he was pushed into their den, a huge stone rolled in front of the entrance, and he was left to become lion supper. But Daniel was still alive in the morning. The lions hadn't lost their appetites. God had intervened. Daniel said God sent an angel who shut the lions' mouths. In other words, God had brought him through the trial (Daniel 6).

Paul spoke more than once of being helped by God's power. He listed all the troubles and hardships he'd suffered, and there were plenty, ranging from being stoned to being shipwrecked to being betrayed by false Christians (2 Cor. 11:23–9). Those difficulties and disasters took their toll on Paul, and he was left feeling weak (v.30). But he learned that his weakness was his greatest strength, for it allowed the power of God to come through. 'He said to me, "My grace is sufficient for you, for my power is made perfect in weakness." Therefore I will boast all the more gladly about my weaknesses, so that Christ's power may rest on me. That is why, for Christ's sake, I delight in weaknesses, in insults, in hardships, in persecutions, in difficulties. For when I am weak, then I am strong' (2 Cor. 12:9–10). Because Paul really believed that, he didn't panic when the way was all uphill. He knew he'd always get there. 'I can do everything through him who gives me strength' (Phil. 4:13).

So, logically and biblically, the case is convincing. Christians are cared for by an almighty God who provides for his people's needs. He will allow nothing to come into their lives greater than they can bear.

'Sinking under the pressure'

Yet get below the evangelical smiles, and you find many Christians aren't coping. Ask, 'How are you?' and they tell you they're 'fine'. But they're not. (In our church we now assume the answer 'fine' means 'Feeling Inadequate, Needing Encouragement'.) Stresses of work or family, emotional trauma from a difficult or broken relationship, pain from past experiences, fears about the future, doubts and depression, these and many other things are often beyond what people can bear. Women and young adults are the most likely to admit they're struggling, but it's true of all ages and all types. They pray, claim answers by faith, try their best, but still they're not making it. They tell me, 'I'm a Christian. I ought to be able to handle these things. But I can't. I'm sinking under the pressure.'

Some sink right under, and the consequences can be terrible. A young woman killed herself because she couldn't cope any longer with the stresses she felt inside. Several others have attempted suicide. These are all Christians. For most, there's nothing so dramatic, just a gradual slide into depression, apathy, loss of faith or self-recrimination. One of them shrugs his shoulders and says, 'I asked God to help me, but nothing happened. I struggled on until I couldn't manage any more.' Another blames himself: 'Obviously I didn't pray enough, or trust enough in the Lord. If I had, I would have had the strength to go on.'

What's gone wrong for these people? Has God let them down? When times got tough, did God not deliver on his promises? Or is the problem with them? Have they not relied on God as they should?

The answer is neither of those options. They've caved in because they expected something from God unpromised by him – personal strength to overcome any difficulty – and therefore they never used the resource he had already provided for them.

False premise

Let's dispose of the myth and then move to reality.

The premise that God will never allow anything into our lives greater than we can bear is false. The Bible does not teach that individual omnipotence over all problems is part of the blessings of salvation.

But doesn't it say that God is faithful, and will allow no hardship to come to you greater than you can bear? No, it doesn't. Those who think it does usually have 1 Corinthians 10:13 in mind: 'No temptation has seized you except what is common to man. And God is faithful; he will not let you be tempted beyond what you can bear. But when you are tempted, he will also provide a way out so that you can stand up under it.' The verse concerns moral temptation. Some equate being tempted with being tested, hence God will enable the Christian to survive any time of testing: any stress, hardship or pressure. But 1 Corinthians 10:13 isn't referring to stress, hardship or pressure, and isn't guaranteeing rescue from problems. Paul was writing about the sins of idolatry and immorality, and wanted his readers to know there was no temptation so great they'd

have to give in to it. There would always be a way out.
By reassuring them that sin could always be avoided, he
stripped them of any excuse for indulging in sin. Now, that
was Paul's message to them: God will never allow you to
face an irresistible temptation. He certainly wasn't saying
that an individual Christian will be given divine strength
to overcome every difficulty.

Surely, though, that is the meaning behind Paul's claim
in Philippians 4:13 that he could do everything through God
who gave him strength? It sounds like a confident testimony
to being able to face any and all hardships in God's power.
Nothing was impossible, for nothing was beyond him and
God together.

But Paul's words need qualification.

No claim to personal omnipotence

First, only the dumbest literalist would take him to be
claiming personal omnipotence. Could Paul flap his arms
and fly like a bird? Could Paul outsprint a cheetah? Could
Paul blast into space and visit the moon? Could Paul claim
God's strength for *anything*?

Of course God can do whatever he pleases, and, if he
wanted, he could make Paul fly, or run at 50 m.p.h. or
become a spaceman. In that simplistic sense, though, that
wasn't what Paul was saying. He knew very well there
were things which, barring some miracle, he couldn't do.
After all, while he was writing or dictating these lines he
was chained in prison (Phil. 1:13). He couldn't merely
throw off his shackles and walk free. His imprisonment
might be ended by a death sentence. If so he wouldn't
be immune to the thrust of the executioner's sword. He'd
seen others die, and, in his former life as a Pharisee, been
responsible for some of those deaths. They hadn't escaped.
Though they were fine Christians, they suffered. And Paul
had suffered too. He'd been through lashings, shipwrecks,
hunger, sleeplessness and much more. He was no masochist.

These were not experiences he welcomed. They hurt, and he didn't want them to happen. But there had never been a 'magic prayer' to make any of them go away. He had to endure them.

In other words, Paul knew very well that pain and problems cannot simply be swept aside. When he wrote, 'I can do everything through him who gives me strength,' he didn't mean a Christian can rise above every difficulty merely by claiming God's power.

When Paul said that he could do everything through God's strength, he was stating something both small and great. It was small inasmuch as it was an admission that he could do only what God gave power to do. Daniel was thrown to lions and lived; other children of God were thrown to lions and died. No Christian could do anything of spiritual significance unless the sovereign God provided strength. Yet his statement was also great, for it was a declaration that God's power was at work. Paul's ministry was far more than one man's achievements, far greater than what sharp intellect, persuasive argument or dynamic leadership could accomplish. People were being saved and churches being planted because God was pouring out his power through Paul. Marvellous things were being done because of God. In that sense Paul was doing everything through him who gave him strength.

Paul's words were a legitimate boast that God was using a weak man. They were not a claim that that man was immune to all hardships.

Support through others

Second, the strength Paul received from God did not drop out of the sky. Most of the time Paul's needs were met through the people of God.

In his letters, including Philippians 4, Paul often talks about fellow Christians helping him. 'I rejoice greatly in the Lord that at last you have renewed your concern for me. Indeed, you have been concerned, but you had no opportunity to show it' (Phil. 4:10). That's a reference – delicately worded – to the fact that they'd sent him money. Finance becomes explicit later. 'When I set out from Macedonia, not one church shared with me in the matter of giving and receiving, except you only; for even when I was in Thessalonica, you sent me aid again and again when I was in need' (Phil. 4:15–16). Notice Paul's last four words: he was in need. How was his need met? The Philippians sent him money, and that wasn't for the first time. They were regular financial backers of Paul's ministry. For a little while support had been impossible, but now they were able to get gifts to him again.

When they hadn't been able to do much for Paul financially, one of their church members had gone to be his personal assistant. Paul thanked the Philippians for Epaphroditus 'whom you sent to take care of my needs' (Phil. 2:25). Epaphroditus' work had been important, and he'd almost paid the ultimate price to do it. Paul told them: 'Welcome him in the Lord with great joy, and honour men like him, because he almost died for the work of Christ, risking his life to make up for the help you could not give me' (Phil. 2:29–30).

Epaphroditus' assistance was merely one small part of a whole package of support Paul got for his work. Many of his letters have references to aid from other Christians. The final chapter of his letter to the Romans lists some of the people who, in different ways, made it possible for him to carry out his commission:

- Phoebe: 'a great help to many people, including me' (Rom. 16:2).
- Priscilla and Aquila: 'my fellow-workers in Christ Jesus. They risked their lives for me' (Rom. 16:3–4).
- Rufus' mother: 'who has been a mother to me, too' (Rom. 16:13).
- Timothy: 'my fellow-worker' (Rom. 16:21).

- Gaius: 'whose hospitality I and the whole church here enjoy' (Rom. 16:23).

These people were all involved with Paul's ministry, some in the background meeting his needs, others beside him in the cut and thrust of first-century evangelism.

Then, of course, there were Barnabas and Silas who are portrayed in Acts as Paul's closest companions. Barnabas stood shoulder to shoulder with Paul during the early days of ministry. Later Silas took his place. Both shared the best and worst of his experiences: the joy of conversions, the excitement of miracles, the pain of persecution, the disappointment of desertions. For example, who was it in Philippi who was attacked by the crowd, severely flogged, thrown into prison, fastened in the stocks, survived an earthquake which burst open the prison's doors and broke the prisoners' chains, and which led to the conversion of the jailer and his family? That wasn't just Paul, but Paul *and* Silas. They were together through it all. Paul wrote about 'the hardships *we* suffered . . . *We* were under great pressure, far beyond *our* ability to endure, so that *we* despaired even of life. Indeed, in *our* hearts *we* felt the sentence of death' (2 Cor. 1:8–9). The plural references are clear.

The point is this. Certainly Paul had strength from God, but most of the time that strength was channelled through people God put alongside Paul. Some of them strengthened him by their distant support, their prayers and their gifts. Some strengthened him by their encouragement and hospitality when he passed their way. Some strengthened him by walking the roads with him, sharing the work, being beside him through good times and bad.

Part of a family

What stares us in the face from Paul's life is that God's help in hard times is channelled through his people. When we become children of God, we don't merely get a Father but also a family. We acquire brothers and sisters, and God means us to provide for each other's needs.

By giving and receiving, Paul modelled that. He also taught it. 'Carry each other's burdens, and in this way you will fulfil the law of Christ' (Gal. 6:2). That statement is simple logic – a burden shared between two is half as heavy as that burden carried by one.

But there's something deeper than just that for, Paul said, sharing burdens fulfils Christ's law. He may have been thinking of specific words of Jesus about sharing, such as, 'Freely you have received, freely give' (Matt. 10:8). Or he may have been referring to Christ's example. We know he did much for others: '. . . the Son of Man did not come to be served, but to serve' (Matt. 20:28). What we think of less is what others did for him. He needed the companionship and practical help of quite a number. 'Jesus travelled about from one town and village to another, proclaiming the good news of the kingdom of God. The Twelve were with him, and also some women who had been cured of evil spirits and diseases . . . These women were helping to support them out of their own means' (Luke 8:1–3). So, the pattern Christ set was helping others and accepting help from others. He taught sharing and practised it. Likewise, then, his disciples should share the burdens of others.

Part of a body

In fact Paul saw mutual support as more than merely a law or act of kindness. It's an inevitability for God's people, because the Church is more than merely a family.

Every member of a family is interrelated, but not necessarily interdependent. Children need their parents when they're small, but when they grow up they usually spread their wings. They make their own decisions, live by their own standards, form their own relationships. They're still related to their parents, but (hopefully) don't rely on them. Paul saw the bonds between Christians as stronger than that, and therefore chose a metaphor with implications deeper than those of a family: the body. 'The body is not made up of one part but of many. The eye cannot say to the hand, "I don't need you!" And the head cannot say to the feet, "I don't need you!" If one part suffers, every part suffers with it; if one part is honoured, every part rejoices with it' (1 Cor. 12:14, 21, 26). Every part of the body is closely linked to and relies on every other part of the body. Paul then added, 'Now you are the body of Christ, and each one of you is a part of it' (1 Cor. 12:27). Put another way, he's saying Christians are not only interrelated but also interdependent.

The significance of that is immense, varied and very relevant to the issue of coping with problems and pressures. It means one part of the body of Christ should not try to carry burdens which need many parts of the body to take that amount of strain. My fireside chair is heavy, and I struggle to move it. I certainly can't lift it with one hand like I would one of our lightweight dining chairs. So if I need to shift the fireside chair, my arms go round it, my back is coiled and my legs braced, and the whole of my body combines to hoist it up. That's how it's meant to be in the body of Christ. Small problems, the routine irritants or responsibilities of life, we manage by ourselves (like my hand alone can carry small objects). But crises, major decisions or severe pressures we can't cope with alone, nor are we meant to. This has nothing to do with how sanctified someone is – a holier person won't do any better – for God's strategy to get any of us through tough times is for us to find the combined strength of the body of Christ.

Too many have struggled unnecessarily. Some say, 'I can manage. I don't need anyone else.' That's pride. Most say, 'Surely all I have to do is pray, and God's strength is mine.' That's bad theology. God's power cannot be privatised. Almost always his help comes through the body of Christ. Those who are determined to get by independently will often crack under the strain.

Needing others

When we look more fairly at the Scriptures we find that God's servants have always needed others, for example Moses, Job and even Jesus.

Moses was sent back to Egypt to set his people free, but was told to take his brother Aaron as companion and spokesman. Later, after the freedom march had begun, he had to have even more help. Moses was judge for the people's quarrels. Day after day, from morning until night, he told them God's law for their disputes. His father-in-law, Jethro, saw a problem.

What you are doing is not good. You and these people who come to you will only wear yourselves out. The work is too heavy for you; you cannot handle it alone. Listen now to me and I will give you some advice, and may God be with you. You must be the people's representative before God and bring their disputes to him. Teach them the decrees and laws, and show them the way to live and the duties they are to perform. But select capable men from all the people – men who fear God, trustworthy men who hate dishonest gain – and appoint them as officials over thousands, hundreds, fifties and tens. Have them serve as judges for the people at all times, but have them bring every difficult case to you; the simple cases they can decide themselves. That will make your load lighter, because they will share it with you. If you do this and God so commands, you will be able to stand the strain, and all these people will go home satisfied. (Exod. 18:17–23)

Moses took his father-in-law's advice, and shared out the work. That eased the pressure, and he was able to continue being leader of the people. If he hadn't, if he'd simply prayed more and battled on alone, he'd have cracked under the long-term physical and mental stress.

A *lack* of encouragement and support made Job's sufferings worse than they might have been. His farming empire had been stolen or destroyed, his children had died suddenly, and he'd been afflicted from head to foot with a severe skin condition. In terrible physical and mental pain, he was abandoned by most. Here's his own description:

> My kinsmen have gone away; my friends have forgotten me. My guests and my maidservants count me a stranger; they look upon me as an alien. I summon my servant, but he does not answer, though I beg him with my own mouth. My breath is offensive to my wife; I am loathsome to my own brothers. Even the little boys scorn me; when I appear, they ridicule me. All my intimate friends detest me; those I love have turned against me. I am nothing but skin and bones; I have escaped by only the skin of my teeth. (Job 19:14–20)

Three friends did come to console Job, but most of the time they lectured and accused him. They plumbed new depths of ineffectiveness in helping him through his crisis, and Job didn't hesitate to tell them several times how useless they were: 'A despairing man should have the devotion of his friends, even though he forsakes the fear of the Almighty. But my brothers are as undependable as intermittent streams . . . You are worthless physicians, all of you! If only you would be altogether silent! For you, that would be wisdom. Miserable comforters are you all! Will your long-winded speeches never end?' (Job 6:14–15, 13:4–5; 16:2–3). So bad were they, anyone today who's an outright failure at helping a troubled person is known as a 'Job's comforter'.

Therefore Job went through his experience with no effective support. How did that leave him? Very desolate:

- 'If only my anguish could be weighed and all my misery be placed on the scales! It would surely outweigh the sand of the seas – no wonder my words have been impetuous' (Job 6:2–3).
- 'I loathe my very life; therefore I will give free rein to my complaint and speak out in the bitterness of my soul' (Job 10:1).
- 'My spirit is broken, my days are cut short, the grave awaits me' (Job 17:1).
- 'The churning inside me never stops; days of suffering confront me' (Job 30:27).

What Job needed were friends to stand alongside him, give him real comfort and share his troubles. With that he might not have been so bitter, nor felt his agony so keenly. Denied help, he nearly didn't survive.

Even Jesus struggled when the companionship and backing he wanted weren't given. He came to Gethsemane knowing that to go on was to be killed. Crucifixion was so horrific and so cruel, the Romans didn't use it on their own citizens. Jesus, fully man as well as fully God, recoiled from going to the cross, overcome with sadness and distress. So he took the three disciples to whom he was closest, and told them, 'My soul is overwhelmed with sorrow to the point of death. Stay here and keep watch with me' (Matt. 26:38). But they didn't keep watch. They fell asleep, and Christ was terribly alone during dark moments of fighting to go forward with what he knew was the will of the Father. Yet he wasn't quite alone. Not even the Son of God could come through this experience by himself, so he was given companionship, as Luke records: 'An angel from heaven appeared to him and strengthened him' (Luke 22:43). Whether the angel laid hands on him, knelt beside him or did something else, we don't know. But he was there. Jesus needed him to be there. Even then, the struggle was immense. 'And being in anguish, he prayed more earnestly, and his sweat was like drops of blood falling to the ground'

(Luke 22:44). But Jesus survived – 'not my will, but yours be done' (v.42) was his conclusion – and rose from his knees to face arrest, trial and crucifixion.

No one can presume on being given angelic company. For support through times of trouble, most of us don't need it for we have the rest of the body of Christ around us, people who love us and will share our burdens.

Christians need each other

Burden-sharing requires care to be offered from one side and accepted from the other. Often relationships between Christians aren't close enough for that to work. Stage one of being ready to cope in times of trouble, then, is strengthening links with others. Stage two is honesty. Even with these in place, it's hard. We're used to pretending we're 'fine'; instead we'll have to admit we have weaknesses. We don't like to be dependent on anyone; instead we'll have to rely on the wisdom and strength of others. We want to get on with our own busy schedules; instead we'll have to make time for the needs of others. But that's the Christian life.

My hand functions because it's supplied with life from the rest of the body. If it was chopped off, it would be useless and dead. Christians need each other in the body of Christ just as much as my hand needs the rest of my body. The support of fellow Christians is the way God's power will reach them when things come into their lives greater than they can bear. If, through pride or faulty thinking, some imagine they can get by alone, they sever themselves from the body. Because their own resources aren't enough, they soon feel weak and life withers.

I'm grateful I'd learned my need of others before a major crisis came. The crisis was to find myself slowly drowning in a sea of depression. I seemed to be sinking deeper and deeper, until all light seemed to have gone and I lived in darkness. Sometimes I felt sad; more often my world was simply drained of colour. Nothing, especially myself, seemed to have any worth. I was a failure, had always been a failure and would always be a failure. Anyone who told me I wasn't was merely humouring me. They said there's a light at the end of every dark tunnel. I could see no light at the end of my tunnel. There was nothing worth living for.

I nearly didn't survive that time. The fact that I did is due largely to two people. One is Alison my wife, who loved me as much through the bad times as she had through the good; the other, Jim, who had supported and helped me for years, sacrificing much to care for me.

Neither Alison nor Jim had 'magic' words to tell me that changed my way of thinking. Rather, they gave me four simple things. The first was acceptance. Even when I was being hostile, they put up with me. They cared for the depressed miserable person I was. I didn't have to become better before they loved me; they loved me as I was. That really mattered. The second thing was support. There were late-night phone calls, time given for meetings, listening to my feelings, helping me with practical tasks I couldn't face. Sometimes Alison would just lie in bed beside me and hold my hand. The third thing was perspective. The world I saw was sad and hopeless. They assured me there was more to the world than what I saw. And because I trusted and respected them, I believed what they said. That didn't change anything instantly, but it kept me going when otherwise I might have given up. The fourth thing was hope. I lost count of the number of times Jim told me, 'You won't always feel like this.' Both assured me there was a life beyond depression, something worth living for. And their words proved true.

What would have happened if I hadn't had Alison and Jim? No one can answer a question like that. I might have made it, but I don't know how.

What I do know is that that depression was something God allowed into my life greater than I could bear. I couldn't get through it alone. I didn't have to. I leaned on those God gave me, and together we made it. In the body of Christ there is strength to face what can't be faced alone.

15

What we must have is a vision

Revd Bill Scott was in trouble. His congregation, or at least some of them, didn't think he was spiritual enough. He was a good man: friendly, hard-working and well-educated. But he kept wanting to do things without finding out first if they were what God wanted him to do.

For example, there was the evangelism programme. Bill kept preaching that they ought to share their faith at every opportunity. Worse, he wanted as many as possible to get basic training in how to witness. He'd even suggested some might go to homes near their church and talk to the people who lived there about Christ. It was too much. And they'd told him. 'Has *God* said to us that's what we're to do? If he's not given us that specific vision, we can't go ahead.'

Evangelism wasn't the only problem. He'd wanted to start a lunch club because there were so many elderly people in the area. Some needed a decent meal while others were lonely and company would do them good. Then there had been hints that the church ought to care for the unemployed. With more than twenty-five per cent out of work in the area, he'd said there was surely something the church should do to help them find meaning for their lives, perhaps even to help them find employment.

His ideas for youth were the most disturbing of all. Teenagers hung around the doorway of the church, and Bill had been told by the church board to make them move on, away from the church premises. But, blow it, rather than ordering them bluntly to take their ideas of vandalism elsewhere, he'd got into conversation with them, asked what the church could do for them, and then come back with their request for a club where they could have fun and meet their friends. He'd put the idea into his pastoral letter in the church magazine, and before Sunday was past five people had offered to run it because they'd been concerned about the local youngsters for a long time.

Now he was telling the church they ought to care for their neighbours, that there were sick people they should visit and pray for, and that it wasn't right that just two adults were left to teach the twenty youngsters who were in Sunday School.

This couldn't go on. A few of the board gathered in secret, and then summoned Bill to meet with them.

'Bill,' the chairman said, 'we have something to say to you in love.'

Bill's heart sank. It must be serious.

'It's good you have so much energy and so many ideas. Nothing wrong in principle with that. But a church needs to be led in a more spiritual way.' Knowing looks were exchanged between the members of the board, halos of holiness hovering over their heads.

'I'm not sure I understand what you mean,' said Bill quietly.

That confession confirmed their worst fears. It seemed a long pause before someone said, 'Let's take this youth club business, Bill. We can't start something like that unless God tells us. Church history is littered with good ideas which weren't God's ideas.' The speaker smiled. He liked that turn of phrase.

'But I have all the guidance I need to love youngsters and share the gospel with them. Those kids will never come to one of our services, so I have to get close to them some other way if I'm ever to talk to them about Christ. The club will let me do that, and I have five gifted people who are willing to make it happen.'

'Yes, Bill. If God tells us that *those* youngsters are the

ones we've to reach, and that *this* type of club is the one we've to run, that's fine. But if your plan isn't from God it'll all come to nothing. We can't start this unless God gives us a clear vision for it.'

The conversation moved on to the other new ventures, and the board's view was unvarying. They could pray for sick people only if God showed them those were the sick people he wanted to heal; they could visit lonely people only if those were the ones God meant them to have a special ministry towards; they could run a lunch club only if that was God's particular way for them to care for the elderly. Same with the rest. It all came down to having the right specific vision.

'It's what the Bible teaches, Bill – you should know that,' someone else said with more than a hint of reproach in her voice. She'd looked up her Bible before the meeting, memorised her proof text, and now quoted it emphatically and triumphantly: 'Proverbs 29:18, "Where there is no vision, the people perish."'

There was silence for a time. A weariness born of months of hard work pressed down on Bill. So much effort, so little appreciation.

The board chairman sensed Bill's sadness and tiredness, and tried to sound positive. 'Bill, instead of putting challenges and tasks before us one after another, just bring us closer to God. Then we'll discover his vision for our church. Once we know that, we'll see marvellous things taking place. We won't have to strive to make them happen. God's power will fall, people will believe, and we'll have revival. Doesn't that sound wonderful, Bill? But we have to do things God's way, so we can't begin on any work until we know what that is. We must wait until he gives us his vision.'

'That's right. We can't make it happen, and we can't hurry it on,' another board member said, basking in his wisdom. 'Remember what the Scripture teaches in Habakkuk 2:3 about getting a vision, "though it tarry, wait for it."'

Something snapped inside Bill, and he struggled to keep control. 'This church has been declining for years waiting for a vision. We're asking God to tell us what he's already told us. Most of what God wants is plain and obvious, and we just need to get on with doing it. People are going to a lost eternity while we sit around pretending to be spiritual.'

There was a sharp intake of breath from across the room. Bill sensed he'd gone too far, yet he felt better for saying what he'd been thinking for ages.

'We're sorry you look on it like that, pastor.' Bill noted it wasn't his name but his title which was being used now. 'We don't want to oppose you, but we can't allow this church to be led away from God.'

With that the board members got up to leave. Clearly the meeting was over. Bill had a hundred more things to say, but he wasn't to be given the chance. He knew it probably wouldn't make any difference anyway.

As they left the room, one turned back towards him. 'I'm disappointed in you, pastor. I thought you were more of a man of God.' Then she left.

The youth club idea was voted out at the next board meeting. No evangelism programme was ever approved. Nor did a lunch club get started, nor anything for the unemployed, nor did anyone else assist with the Sunday School. There was a lot of waiting for a vision. There was not a lot of anything else.

Within six months Bill resigned, dejected and disillusioned. Many dreams, but little chance or help to see them happen.

Within six years the church closed. Not enough members were left to carry on. The vision had tarried longer than most of the members had lived.

Revd Bill Scott may have lacked tact. He may have lacked resilience. He may have lacked the ability to involve his people in formulating plans. But would any number of fine words, any amount of superhuman patience or any degree of management skill have overcome the fundamental resistance of his board members who wouldn't budge unless heaven opened and God spoke personally and specifically about what they were to do as a church?

An increasing number would argue that his board members were right. If Christ is the head of his Church then it's his will which matters, not our best plans. If anything of eternal value is to be done, then it will be in his power, not with our greatest strength.

Doing things God's way

Hasn't it always been a case of finding God's way?

The first Christians were initially banned from doing evangelism. 'On one occasion, while he was eating with them, he gave them this command: "Do not leave Jerusalem, but wait for the gift my Father promised, which you have heard me speak about. For John baptised with water, but in a few days you will be baptised with the Holy Spirit" ' (Acts 1:4–5). Temporarily, Jesus stopped his disciples carrying out the commission he'd given them. In case they tried to do his work in their own power, he ordered them not to take a step outside Jerusalem until they had the Holy Spirit. At Pentecost the Spirit fell on them, and then out into the streets they went. A crowd gathered, and the gospel was told. Evangelism was done. The disciples would never have thought of worshipping God in the street at 9 a.m. using unknown languages. They would never have dared preach openly about Jesus so soon after his crucifixion. This method of evangelism wasn't their choice. But that's the point. It was *God's* choice, and therefore very effective. On that first day of witness, doing things God's way, some three thousand were converted and baptised. It was the outworking of an old truth: ' "Not by might nor by power, but by my Spirit," says the LORD Almighty' (Zech. 4:6). God's work would never be done by man's enterprise, no matter how clever it was.

Paul taught that too. He wrote, 'We live by faith, not by

sight' (2 Cor. 5:7). That was his own experience, something he had had to learn the hard way. Acts 16 relates how Paul became uncertain where he should go next on his missionary travels. His original plan of moving into Asia had been stopped by the Holy Spirit, so, instead, he'd gone through Phrygia and Galatia until he reached the border of Mysia. At that point Paul thought he could simply press forward in the obvious direction, but he was wrong.

> When they came to the border of Mysia, they tried to enter Bithynia, but the Spirit of Jesus would not allow them to. So they passed by Mysia and went down to Troas. During the night Paul had a vision of a man of Macedonia standing and begging him, 'Come over to Macedonia and help us.' After Paul had seen the vision, we got ready at once to leave for Macedonia, concluding that God had called us to preach the gospel to them. (Acts 16:7–10)

Twice in a short space of time Paul was prevented from doing what he thought best because God had other ideas. Eventually he got God's vision – to go into Macedonia – and so began a new and significant phase in the spread of the gospel. It was God's way, and doing things God's way was the key to power in Paul's work.

Much of today's Church thinks the way to success is to adopt the best of business methods, tap the expertise of entrepreneurs, draw up a five-year plan, and (sometimes) promote a new and trendy image. Mostly these things haven't worked, for what the Church really needed was not the best agenda man could devise but the agenda God had appointed for it. There might be nothing clever, nothing sophisticated, nothing impressive about God's way. But it would be the way God would bless.

So, the need is to scrap most of our complex and demanding programmes and get back to seeking God. When we find him and get our vision from him, then, and only then, dare the Church move forward. When God has made clear what's to be done, when we're sure of his will, then we can press on confident that we'll see mighty works and a great harvest.

That sounds great. Who would want to argue with it? Yet, far from being the sure-fire way to blessing, that apparently spiritual logic can be a massive block to getting God's work done.

Christian paralysis

The origins of ideas which sound so spiritual don't always (to use a phrase) lie on the right side of the tracks.

If I were the devil, and I couldn't destroy Christians or persuade them not to witness or work for Christ, what tactic would be left to me? I'd tell them, 'Don't do it now. There will be a better time than now.' How could I persuade them of that? I'd whisper in their ears that they ought to be *sure* of God's will, that they ought to have a clear vision for what they have to do, and they need that *before* they start. It would be sin to go forward without a God-given blueprint detailing specifically what he wants done.

What a demonic version of me would aim for is a subtle reversal of 2 Corinthians 5:7. Instead of walking by faith and not by sight, I'd persuade people to walk by sight and not by faith. I'd lean on two particular insecurities. One is the dread of not perfectly pleasing God, and the other is the fear that people will ridicule or get hostile if we witness to them. The answer to both kinds of insecurity is certainty. I'd play on that. I'd make them believe they were entitled to certainty, certainty about being exactly in God's will, and certainty that their witness will be effective at minimum cost. Of course, what would follow would be an endless search. No one can ever have absolute assurances about God's will, and God will never promise to make witnessing and working for Christ easy. They'll never find certainty. Therefore they'll never actually do anything. By telling them they must have a clear vision from God I'd paralyse them.

Whether Satan plays on our insecurities, or our fears are enough by themselves, the result is today's Christian doesn't want to walk by faith but by sight. He needs every last detail in place so he's sure exactly what's going to happen. He can't face a plan that lacks guarantees or a future which is undefined.

Overcoming insecurities

Thankfully the biblical heroes overcame their insecurities. They had them, sometimes in abundance, but that didn't stop them going forward. Their futures were undefined and the precise will of God unclear but they did the work anyway.

Abraham was like that. God sent him off with few explicit details: 'Leave your country, your people and your father's household and go to the land I will show you' (Gen. 12:1). Apart from promises of blessing, Abraham had little else. Yet he went. Did he get better guidance soon? It seems not, for there's no record of God speaking to him again until he got to the land of Canaan. 'The LORD appeared to Abram and said, "To your offspring I will give this land." So he built an altar there to the LORD, who had appeared to him' (Gen. 12:7). Abraham didn't sit still in Haran until God gave him a blueprint of all that lay ahead; he went forward on the leading he had and only when he got where he was supposed to be was he given more. For all that, much was vague, and chapter after chapter of Genesis relates his journeys up and down the land, and even (disobediently) back over its border. Plenty of times Abraham wasn't sure of God's will. But, in general, he got on with the little he knew, and so became the father of God's people.

Did Moses have an easier time? He had a very dramatic encounter with God at a burning bush, and he was told exactly what God wanted him to do. Well, he was and he wasn't.

> The LORD said, 'I have indeed seen the misery of my people in Egypt. I have heard them crying out because of their slave drivers, and I am concerned about their suffering. So I have come down to rescue them from the hand of the Egyptians and to bring them up out of that land into a good and spacious land, a land flowing with milk and honey – the home of the Canaanites, Hittites, Amorites, Perizzites, Hivites and Jebusites. And now the cry of the Israelites has reached me, and I have seen the way the Egyptians are oppressing them. So now, go. I am sending you to Pharaoh to bring my people the Israelites out of Egypt.' (Exod. 3:7–10)

Precise instructions? The will of God clear? Yes, but where are the 'how to' details? Moses' general orders were sharply enough defined, but he wasn't abundantly supplied with particulars how he, a man wanted on a capital charge, could march back into the Egyptian court, successfully negotiate the release of millions of valuable slaves, then simply walk them out of the country, through inhospitable desert, past hostile peoples, and lead them into a land already 'the home of the Canaanites, Hittites, Amorites, Perizzites, Hivites and Jebusites'. It's small wonder that Moses initially declined the job remit. He raised question after question, and though he got many reassurances, Moses remained highly sceptical about the practicability of the task and about his suitability for it. Finally God got angry with Moses and ended the debate. Moses, riddled with doubt, resigned himself to the work, and made a start on one of the most major and most risky leadership jobs in all history. There was so much he didn't know. But he had to get on with it anyway.

The anointing of David as king of Israel is another account of one of God's people having to do a job with little in the way of advance details. Samuel was sent by

God to anoint a son of Jesse of Bethlehem as king. He was to invite Jesse to a sacrifice and then God would show him what to do and which son to anoint (1 Sam. 16:3). Those and only those were his instructions. There was no up-front master plan, just the promise that if he got started on the task more detail would be given when he needed it. Samuel obeyed, and felt hopeful of a good result when Jesse put his sons on parade for they were strong and good-looking fellows. One of them would be perfect for the job. Encouragingly God spoke to him again. Discouragingly it was to tell him none of the seven sons who stood there was the right man. Samuel was puzzled. Maybe Jesse had another son? He did, but he was the youngest and out tending the sheep. Samuel had him brought in, God whispered in his heart that he was the man, and Samuel anointed him with oil (1 Sam. 16:13).

Our familiarity with that story blinds us to the difficulties facing Samuel. He was given scant information before he began, and had lots of uncertainties along the way. He almost anointed the wrong son (1 Sam. 16:6)! But those difficulties and uncertainties weren't Samuel's fault. They weren't because he was failing to have faith. The very opposite of that was true. His faith was precisely what had allowed him to go forward even when he wasn't sure what to do. God could have given him a charismatic word of knowledge about the name David before he started. But God didn't. Samuel had to begin with the meagre data he had, and trust for more particulars later.

Biblical heroes like Abraham, Moses and Samuel didn't have flowcharts revealed to them. Plans, timetables and drawings weren't dropped from heaven, complete with sets of instructions on how to accomplish each stage. Probably they longed for a 'painting by numbers' method to achieve an acceptable outcome from their near impossible tasks, some kind of guarantee they'd get God's will done. But they had no such luxury. All they knew was the *next* thing they had to do. When that was done, they were told the next, and so on. The Bible is full of people who, for one reason or another, had to do God's work with uncertainties.

Struggling and stumbling

Some didn't cope easily with that, and it made them want to quit. Gideon was almost always unsure of God's will, probably because his own sense of inadequacy clashed with what God asked of him. 'But Lord,' Gideon asked, 'how can I save Israel? My clan is the weakest in Manasseh, and I am the least in my family' (Judg. 6:15). Uncertainty brooded over every step he took. Elijah swayed between massive confidence and paralysing fear. On Mount Carmel his trust in God peaked as he challenged the prophets of Baal to a test that would show which God could send down fire from heaven to light a sacrifice (1 Kings 18:19–40). Days later it nose-dived when his life was threatened, and he ran away into the desert. 'He came to a broom tree, sat down under it and prayed that he might die. "I have had enough, LORD," he said. "Take my life; I am no better than my ancestors"' (1 Kings 19:4). Elijah scaled the heights of faith and plumbed the depths of doubt. It wasn't easy for him to do God's will.

Neither Gideon nor Elijah – great heroes in God's service – always knew exactly what God wanted, nor did they always press forward with confidence that everything would work out. They struggled, really struggled with God's will for them. Sometimes they failed. Mostly they got there, but only with pain.

Who wants pain? No one, of course, and increasingly it's an unacceptable by-product of being a Christian in a comfort-conscious world. Like Revd Scott's congregation, we want to know our evangelism and other work for Christ will be effective without any significant cost to us. A vision seems to offer that. If God will show us (a 'picture') or tell us (a 'word from the Lord') his plan, we can be rid of our uncertainties and make straight for God's will. God's will, of course, promises fulfilment, joy and a sense of victory. (The hardship and sacrifice which are also common with God's will are inconvenient and therefore ignored.) So, if only we can have a vision of what God wants, we have an up-front assurance of success and happiness. Why stumble in the dark when God will give light? Strangely, though, many of the greatest Old Testament figures did a lot of stumbling. Visionary light burned fairly dim for them.

Doing what's obvious

Equally strangely, the New Testament's heroes never expected their light would come from visions.

An unnoticed but significant detail is that not a single person in the New Testament ever sought a vision. Some had visions, even great ones like that of John in the book of Revelation. But no one went searching for one. Paul never aimed to see a man of Macedonia. His concern was to obey the command he had been given to take the gospel to the Gentiles, so he went anywhere there were people who needed to hear of Christ. The vision which called him to Macedonia was unsought, unexpected and unusual. He hadn't looked for it, for normally he didn't need any vision. On this occasion, God wanted to divert him somewhere special and so gave him special guidance.

Paul's norm was to get on and do what was clear and obvious, in obedience to the general commands of God. Today's Church is becoming too much like faint-hearted infantrymen who, rather than fight, prefer to huddle in their trench hoping HQ will radio through some super tactics that will allow them to advance without being hurt. But victory doesn't usually come like that. Soldiers gain ground going over the top and attacking into a hail of bullets. Many do get hurt.

God's victories aren't won either from the safety of a trench. Jesus made no promises of easy advances, and gave his first disciples no risk-free tactics. Many of them suffered;

many died doing Christ's work. The modern Christian has no more right than his first-century predecessor to effortless or painless ways to serve Christ. Nor, any more than the biblical heroes, can he have one hundred per cent sureness of what he's called to do. The norm is one tentative step after another, often hesitantly, often heart in mouth.

It's frequently like walking in fog. The goal is unseen and the best you know is the rough direction in which to head. Visibility is down to ten metres, and there's a risk of walking over the edge of a cliff. But move you must, so you edge forward, peering into the gloom. Sometimes you stumble, sometimes brush against a jagged rock. How you wish the weather would clear, but you can't wait for that because you'll die if you stay where you are. Slowly you walk on, finding encouragement that when you've gone ten metres you can see another ten. After ten more, you see ten more. So you progress. It's not exciting, not quick, and not without accident and failure. But at least you move, and eventually you reach your goal.

No blueprints, but a God who can be trusted

Yet the Bible says that 'where there is no vision, the people perish'. It's not the lack of a specific, crystal clear vision that causes people to perish. They perish when they lose touch with the living God, the God who is to be trusted and obeyed. That's really what the writer of Proverbs 29:18 teaches. Revd Scott's church member preferred to quote the Authorised (King James) Version because it suited his argument. A more modern translation like the New International Version has a slightly different meaning: 'Where there is no revelation, the people cast off restraint . . .' Where they have no consciousness of God, people do what they please, and hence they perish. Our need today is not to see the way ahead. Our need is to 'see' God, to have a fresh vision of him, hear his commands and feel his compassion. Then, knowing him as both our

loving Father and the mighty God, we'll be willing to take
his hand and edge forward. We don't know what's ahead,
but he does. And he can be trusted.

But what about the other Scriptural quotation cited by
one of Revd Scott's board members? Habakkuk said to wait
for God's vision even if it's delayed. Certainly Habakkuk
said that, but he didn't mean what the board member
thought he did. Habakkuk wasn't speaking about getting
a vision or getting clarity about a vision, but about a vision
coming to pass. The revelation given to Habakkuk was
that, because of their sins, his people would be swept
away by the Babylonians. The destruction and misery
caused by that invasion and captivity would be terrible.
But God also showed him that the Babylonians would
not for ever hold his people prisoner. In time disaster
would come on the Babylonians, and God would save
Habakkuk's people. That was a vital revelation and he
was told to write it down because it must not be forgotten
as the years of slavery dragged past. God's reassurance
and promise of rescue must not be lost. Their liberation
might seem a long time coming, but it would happen when
God had ordained. Hence the NIV translation: 'For the
revelation awaits an appointed time; it speaks of the end
and will not prove false. Though it linger, wait for it; it
will certainly come and will not delay' (Hab. 2:3). God was
calling his people to walk by faith and not by sight. He'd
given his word that one day they'd be free, but no detail
how that could come about. To be patient couldn't have
been easy. Being patient with slavery is never easy. But,
by faith, they waited and watched what happened. In time
the Babylonians were overthrown by the Persians, and the
Persians allowed the exiles to return to their own land. God
had never given them a point by point strategy to follow,
and even Habakkuk's revelation had lingered, but it had
come true. They were free.

As in Habakkuk's time, so it is now. We still have to
walk by faith. There's guidance but no blueprint. We don't

know every detail, but we know a God who does. And our vision of him, our trust in him, our obedience to him allow us to move forward, confident that he'll make each of our steps fall in the right direction.

That's been my personal experience. Here's one example.

God and common sense seemed to whisper in our ears that it was time to move house. I was beginning postgraduate studies, so the timing for change was good. With two little children and another due, but not enough rooms for us all, the timing was not only good but necessary. Alison and I had less than no money, but I'd heard that the university had an arrangement for postgraduate students to rent low-cost housing in a nearby new town. An appointment was made at the new town housing department. The assistant gave us a key and told us to check out a property. We needed only a glance to realise it would never do. It was in a block of flats, and its small cramped rooms would imprison a growing family, and destroy any possibility of home study for me. We were disappointed and confused. We'd had a strange feeling God wanted us in that new town. But there was no way we could fit into that flat.

Back to the housing department we went. I explained to the assistant that the place she'd offered was just too small. Taking a deep breath, I asked, 'Would you have anything bigger . . .?' She frowned. 'We never give any properties other than these flats to students.' My heart sank, but I still stood there. 'Hold on, I'll just check something,' she said, and disappeared into a back office. I prayed. She was gone for five minutes. I had prayed a lot before she came back. 'Here's another key. Have a look at that property. It's just become vacant, so we haven't cleaned it up or done maintenance checks on it yet. If you like it, it's yours, but if you don't we won't be able to offer you anything else.'

I gave profuse thanks to her and silently to God, and minds whirring with nervousness and hope, we headed for this unknown location. To our amazement it was a house! Inside were four bedrooms, not to mention living area, dining room, bathroom and kitchen, and all in good order. We were astonished and grateful. Never before had a student been offered a house, and this one seemed perfect for us.

That wasn't the end of the story. We went to the local church, and soon became known there. It turned out the church had reached a strategic moment – thinking of planting a daughter congregation and praying for someone who could give it leadership. Within a year I was the part-time assistant pastor of the church with special responsibility for the brand new daughter congregation. Two years after that I became the first full-time pastor of the now independent new congregation. Three years later we had our own church building, and soon nearly one hundred and fifty members.

I never knew any of that when I stood at the counter in the housing department. All I knew was that we were supposed to be there. It seemed impossible for them to give us adequate housing, but there was a rightness about moving to that town. I had no vision for anything more. But God did. He had a goal, and every detail towards that goal already worked out. He knew exactly what he was doing, and all he needed from me was willingness to take one tentative but obedient step after another, and he'd get me there.

Those who would serve God must get on with what they know now, not wait for the day when they know it all. They must live by faith, not by sight.

Postscript

Evangelical tradition runs strong and deep, and most of the fifteen examples of near Christianity covered in these pages have been part of that tradition for a long time. Like when there's fluoride in water, we've been affected whether we knew it or not, because we've been drinking in their influence day by day. They were so much part of our thinking we assumed the Bible taught these things. Hopefully we're wiser now.

But does the fuss of correcting these myths matter? After all, only the super-arrogant claim a flawless grasp on Christianity. Isn't it good enough, and even a sign of humility, to accept you're only *near* to real Christianity?

Well, is it safe to be near the edge of a cliff? Yes, perfectly safe, unless you're on the wrong side of the edge. Then it's not safe at all.

Being near on the wrong side of truth is as dangerous as stepping over a cliff edge. People mustn't think they're heading for heaven just because they believe the correct facts about Jesus. Nor will the ritual of a quiet time keep them right with God. Nor can they handle any amount of disaster or pressure alone. With these, and all the other subjects, it's serious to get it wrong: people imagine they're saved when they're not, or their relationship with God is good when it isn't, or they can cope when they can't. Real Christianity must arise out of what the Bible actually teaches, not what we'd like it to teach or what we've grown used to thinking it teaches.

If anything written in these pages disillusions you about what you've always believed, remember you can be disillusioned only about illusions. You're better off without illusions, for they're burdens which weigh you down on your spiritual climb. You'll climb better with the solid reality of an uncluttered Christian faith, a faith very worth having.

I hope what's been written here is nearer to the truth than what went before, and, if it's still only near Christianity, I trust it's near on the safer side of the cliff edge.

I had lunch recently with a friend who argued some of these points with me. I kept dragging him back to what the Bible really teaches. 'You're too biblical,' he said finally.

If that's the accusation, I plead guilty.